T0321480

PARALLEL MACHINES: PARALLEL MACHINE LANGUAGES

The Emergence of Hybrid Dataflow Computer Architectures

**THE KLUWER INTERNATIONAL SERIES
IN ENGINEERING AND COMPUTER SCIENCE**

PARALLEL PROCESSING AND
FIFTH GENERATION COMPUTING

Consulting Editor

Doug DeGroot

Other books in the series:

PARALLEL EXECUTION OF LOGIC PROGRAMS
John S. Conery ISBN 0-89838-194-0

PARALLEL COMPUTATION AND COMPUTERS FOR
ARTIFICIAL INTELLIGENCE
Janusz S. Kowalik ISBN 0-89838-227-0

MEMORY STORAGE PATTERNS IN PARALLEL PROCESSING
Mary E. Mace ISBN 0-89838-239-4

SUPERCOMPUTER ARCHITECTURE
Paul B. Schneck ISBN 0-89838-234-4

ASSIGNMENT PROBLEMS IN PARALLEL
AND DISTRIBUTED COMPUTING
Shahid H. Bokhari ISBN 0-89838-240-8

MEMORY PERFORMANCE OF PROLOG ARCHITECTURES
Evan Tick ISBN 0-89838-254-8

DATABASE MACHINES AND KNOWLEDGE BASE MACHINES
Masaru Kitsuregawa ISBN 0-89838-257-2

PARALLEL PROGRAMMING AND COMPILERS
Constantine D. Polychronopoulos ISBN 0-89838-288-2

ANALYSIS OF CACHE PERFORMANCE FOR OPERATING
SYSTEMS AND MULTIPROGRAMMING
Anant Agarwal ISBN 0-7923-9005-9

DATA ORGANIZATION IN PARALLEL COMPUTERS
H.A.G. Wijshoff ISBN 0-89838-304-8

A HIGH PERFORMANCE ARCHITECTURE
FOR PROLOG
T.P. Dobry ISBN 0-7923-9060-1

PARALLEL MACHINES: PARALLEL MACHINE LANGUAGES

The Emergence of Hybrid Dataflow Computer Architectures

by

Robert A. Iannucci
IBM TJ Watson Research Center

with a foreword by

Arvind

KLUWER ACADEMIC PUBLISHERS
Boston/Dordrecht/London

Distributors for North America:
Kluwer Academic Publishers
101 Philip Drive
Assinippi Park
Norwell, Massachusetts 02061, USA

Distributors for all other countries:
Kluwer Academic Publishers Group
Distribution Centre
Post Office Box 322
3300 AH Dordrecht, THE NETHERLANDS

Library of Congress Cataloging-in-Publication Data

Iannucci, Robert A., 1955–
    Parallel machines : parallel machine languages : the emergence of
hybrid dataflow computer architectures / by Robert A. Iannucci.
        p.   cm. — (The Kluwer international series in engineering and
computer science. Parallel processing and fifth generation
computing)
    Includes bibliographical references.
    ISBN 0-7923-9101-2
    1. Parallel computers.   2. Computer architecture.   I. Title.
II. Series.
QA76.5.I12   1990
004 '.35—dc20   90-4151
                                                                               CIP

To Susan, Robbie, and Peter with all my love.

Table of Contents

List of Figures

List of Tables

Foreword

It is universally accepted today that parallel processing is here to stay but that software for parallel machines is still difficult to develop. However, there is little recognition of the fact that changes in processor architecture can significantly ease the development of software. In the seventies the availability of processors that could address a large name space directly, eliminated the problem of name management at one level and paved the way for the routine development of large programs. Similarly, today, processor architectures that can facilitate cheap synchronization and provide a global address space can simplify compiler development for parallel machines. If the cost of synchronization remains high, the programming of parallel machines will remain significantly less abstract than programming sequential machines. In this monograph Bob Iannucci presents the design and analysis of an architecture that can be a better building block for parallel machines than any von Neumann processor.

There is another very interesting motivation behind this work. It is rooted in the long and venerable history of dataflow graphs as a formalism for expressing parallel computation. The field has bloomed since 1974, when Dennis and Misunas proposed a truly novel architecture using dataflow graphs as the parallel machine language. The novelty and elegance of dataflow architectures has, however, also kept us from asking the *real* question: "What can dataflow architectures buy us that von Neumann architectures can't?" In the following I explain in a round about way how Bob and I arrived at this question.

Bob joined my research group in 1981, around the time when we were in the midst of designing an instruction set for a dynamic dataflow architecture based on the U-interpreter. Bob brought to light several important issues that we had forgotten to consider, and proceeded in his usual meticulous, thorough and insightful way to produce the first documentation on the instruction set. Later this architecture came to be known as the Tagged-Token Dataflow Architecture or, simply, the TTDA.

The TTDA specification has served us for many years. As expected, it provided the Id compiler writers with a concrete target language. We began serious discussions about building a TTDA machine but decided against it on the grounds that there were too many unknown parameters, such as the size of the token storage in the waiting-matching unit. However, a group at Electrotechnical Laboratory in Tsukuba, Japan felt no such reticence and, taking the plunge, built the Sigma-1 machine with 128 processors and 128 I-structure storage elements. Operational since January 1988, Sigma-1 represents a very important milestone in dataflow research.

The next step at MIT was to simulate the TTDA on von Neumann machines. This immediately raised the question, At what level of fidelity should the TTDA be simulated? On the one hand, we wanted to examine the gaps in the processor pipeline and, on the other, we needed to study high-level resource management issues. Eventually, we decided to build two "soft" versions of the TTDA for the two different purposes. However, the more we thought about building a fast interpreter, the more confused we became about dataflow computers. Were dataflow graphs merely a convenient formalism for software development, or had they something to say about hardware organization as well?

Bob and I spent almost four years trying to understand what makes a computer a dataflow computer. This exercise began with a hastily written paper titled *A Critique of Multiprocessing von Neumann Style* (for the International Symposium on Computer Architecture held in Stockholm) and culminated in 1987 with the 6th version of this paper entitled *Two Fundamental Issues in Multiprocessing*. Without the wealth of practical knowledge Bob brought from IBM, this paper would have been impossible to write. Bob has presented much of this material in Chapter 1 of this book.

This book represents the continued evolution of these ideas. Can the essence of dataflow architectures be incorporated in von Neumann machines? Bob presents a very interesting design point in this space. His is an architecture that, although only a step away from von Neumann architectures, can execute fine grain dataflow without the loss of significant efficiency over pure dataflow architectures. This book points the direction in which processor architecture must evolve, if we are ever going to have the appropriate hardware base for parallel machines. Without such a base software for parallel machines will remain crippled forever.

Arvind

M.I.T.
Cambridge, Massachusetts
March, 1989

Preface

It has become apparent that the lessons learned in 40 years of designing von Neumann uniprocessors do not necessarily carry over to multiprocessors. Compiler technology coupled with simple pipeline design is now used effectively [35, 47, 48, 50] to cover bounded memory latency in uniprocessors. Unfortunately, the situation is qualitatively different for multiprocessors, where large and often unpredictable latencies in memory and communications systems cannot be tolerated by using similar techniques. This is attributable at the architectural level to poor support for inexpensive dynamic synchronization [8]. Specifically, latency cost is incurred on a per-instruction basis, but synchronization on a per-instruction basis is impractical. A scalable, general purpose multiprocessor architecture must address these issues. Traditional compile time sequencing is too weak a paradigm for general purpose machines (c.f., ELI-512 [28], the ESL Polycyclic processor [49]), and traditional run time sequencing mechanisms are not sufficiently flexible (c.f., The IBM 360 Model 91 [1, 55], the Cray-1 [50]).

Dataflow architectures offer such synchronization at a per-instruction level as the normal *modus operandi*. Each instance of an instruction can be though of as an independent task with specific dependence requirements which must be satisfied prior to initiation. A dataflow machine provides the mechanism to detect efficiently the satisfaction of these requirements and to process all such enabled tasks. Given the means to express a computation as a graph of such interdependent tasks, one has a natural means for executing, at any instant of time, all and only those instructions for which the synchronization constraints have been satisfied. To the extent that the number of such candidate instructions exceeds by some suitable amount the instantaneous capacity of the machine to process them, latencies inherent in the physical machine can be hidden, or masked. Heretofore, seeking these benefits has implied a significant departure from the von Neumann camp of architectures, leaving a very substantial and important body of knowledge behind.

This text presents a framework for understanding the tradeoffs between these two points in the space of computer architectures. The overall goal of this study is to discover the critical hardware structures which must be present in any scalable, general-purpose parallel computer to effectively tolerate latency and synchronization costs. This investigation is based on demonstrating that von Neumann instruction sequencing simplicity and dataflow sequencing generality are but the extrema of a continuum. To explore this continuum, a new architecture is developed as a synthesis of the best features of von Neumann and dataflow ideas. These features are captured in the concept of a parallel machine language which can be grafted on top of an otherwise traditional von Neumann base. In such an architecture, the units of scheduling, called scheduling quanta (SQ's), are bound at compile time rather than at instruction set design time. The parallel machine language supports this notion via a large synchronization name space.

It is shown that the combination of dataflow-style explicit synchronization and von Neumann-style implicit synchronization in the same instruction set results in an architectural synergism. Using an instruction set which is strictly less powerful than that of the MIT Tagged-Token Dataflow Architecture (TTDA), the hybrid architecture can exploit the same kinds of parallelism as the TTDA. Given that a compiler can generate scheduling quanta of two or three instructions, the hybrid architecture will execute approximately the same number of instructions as the TTDA. Larger quanta can result in the hybrid actually executing *fewer* instructions than the TTDA, demonstrating the power of passing state implicitly between program-counter sequenced instructions.

The Problem Domain

Chapter 1 introduces Dataflow Program Graphs, the Two Fundamental Issues of parallel processing, and a framework for reasoning about the cost of parallelism. Dataflow program graphs are motivated on the basis of their expressive power and abstractness. The two fundamental issues are architecture-independent matters of concern within the domain of scalable, general purpose parallel computers. In particular, the desire to switch from a single processor to a connection of many introduces unavoidable latencies. The requirement to similarly decompose a single problem into communicating parts implies the need for efficient, fine-grained synchronization. These issues give rise to a very basic set of economics which relate program parallelism and machine capabilities to measurable costs.

The Importance of Processor Architecture

Chapter 2 examines the strengths and weaknesses of both the von Neumann and dataflow regimes as bases for a parallel computer. In von Neumann architecture, it is shown that the desire to scale a general-purpose machine from the level of tens to thousands of processors implies the need for changes in the basic processor architecture. It is shown that von Neumann machines have only a limited ability to tolerate latency, and little or no ability to provide efficient, fine-grained synchronization.

In a dataflow machine, synchronization is not only available at the lowest hardware levels, it is unavoidable. The key sequencing mechanism in a dataflow machine is based on the matching of names from a large space. Activities, or instances of instructions, are uniquely named. Data for a given instruction are tagged with the activity name. Hardware provides the means for bringing identically-tagged data together and for scheduling the denoted instructions. It is shown that such matching is not strictly necessary in all cases. Moreover, it is shown that in these cases the inability to eliminate such synchronization results in lost locality.

A Dataflow / von Neumann Hybrid

Chapter 3 presents a new architecture which is developed by taking the essential features of a dataflow machine and integrating them into a von Neumann machine. The notion of a parallel machine language is presented which captures the following key features:

- The instruction set is designed in such a way that instruction execution time is always independent of unbounded latencies.

- Synchronization events are named. Names are drawn from a large space, and names can be manipulated as first-class hardware data types.

- Both explicit *and* implicit synchronization can be expressed - programs are represented as partial orders of sequential threads.

Two execution models are presented. The first, an idealized model, captures the notion of executing computations expressed in the parallel machine language, but with few other constraints. The number of processors is assumed to be unbounded, and the communication latency is assumed to be zero. This model provides the means for studying the effects that architectural assumptions have on the behavior of given programs (*e.g.*, the best-case parallelism which can be uncovered). The second model is more realistic. By presenting the high-level design of a realizable processor capable of handling partially-ordered computations, a set of constraints is developed and applied on top of the idealized model. This provides a vehicle for studying and evaluating the efficiency of various implementation devices such as operand caches.

Compiling for the Hybrid Architecture

Chapter 4 considers the issues of compiling code for the hybrid model. In the von Neumann world, compilation is complicated by numerous instances of static resource allocation. Doing a good job of this, however, can result in excellent locality *i.e.*, efficient use of high-bandwidth storage and a solidly packed pipeline. In the dataflow world, many of these problems *cum* opportunities evaporate in the face of implicit management of token storage and the near-zero cost of naming synchronization events. In the hybrid paradigm, compile-time tradeoffs between these two are possible. This significantly complicates the task of generating optimal code.

A simple approach is presented for choosing between these two domains. Dependences between instructions are classed as either static or dynamic, the difference being that a dynamic dependence is sensitive to unbounded latency. Instructions are partitioned into scheduling quanta (SQ's). All instructions in a given SQ depend, transitively, on the same set of dynamic arcs. Having partitioned a computation thus, von Neumann style sequencing is used within an SQ, and dataflow sequencing is used between them. By this means, latency can be masked by excess parallelism as in a dataflow machine.

Analysis

Chapter 5 presents results of emulation experiments run on the idealized and realistic models, using SQ partitioned code derived from Id program graphs. A comparison is made between the hybrid machine and the MIT Tagged-Token Dataflow Architecture (TTDA). In general, it takes two hybrid instructions to equal the computational power of a TTDA instruction. However, it is shown by experimental result that, given the same program graph, the hybrid machine and the TTDA execute approximately the same number of instructions. By this observation it is posited that the full power of TTDA instructions is not used in general, and that a large fraction of this unused power is attributable to unnecessary synchronization generality in the TTDA.

Conclusion

Chapter 6 reviews other related efforts which seek to reconcile, or at least understand, the differences between von Neumann and dataflow architectures. Directions for future research are sketched.

Notation

Within this text, certain notational conventions are followed. Terms being defined in running text appear as DEFINITIONS. Throughout, two levels of instruction set are discussed. The higher level, the Dataflow Program Graph, abstracts away unnecessary detail of the underlying machinery. Instances of instructions from this level appear as **DFPG-OPCODES**. The lower-level is machine specific. Instances of instructions appear as **MACHINE-OPCODES**. Also at this level, machine-specific data types appear as *HARDWARE-TYPES*.

Acknowledgments

This book would not have been possible without the contributions of many individuals. I am especially grateful to my thesis supervisor, Arvind, who coached and encouraged me through seven years and six versions of the *Two Fundamental Issues*. I wish to thank Andrew Chien, David Culler, Bert Halstead, Steve Heller, Greg Papadopoulos, Ken Traub, and other members of the Computation Structures and Parallel Processing Groups for their interest in and enthusiasm for this work. I am grateful to Jack Dennis, Arvind, and Mike Dertouzos for having worked so many years to establish the dataflow research environment of the second floor at Tech Square in which this study was done. I also thank the people of First Presby for their encouragement. In particular, I thank Mike "Rambo" Hale for providing such rewarding (read: time-consuming) distractions from graduate studies, and the Butmans for the use of their lovely cabin at Lake Winnipesaukee where the first draft was written. I also wish to thank Lee Howe, Ev Shimp, Bobby Dunbar, Bill Hoke, Lucie Fjeldstad, Frank Moore, Dick Case, Hum Cordero, Bob Corrigan, Carl Conti, John Karakash and my other sponsors at IBM who made this work possible.

Thanks go to Arvind, Steve Gregor, Kei Hiraki, Paul Suhler, and Ken Traub for their careful proofreading of various versions of this manuscript.

Special thanks go to Stan Brosky, Eleanore Getchy, Alice Otto, and John Schmied who each had a very special and profound influence on the development of my interests in computer science.

I am grateful to my parents and family, especially to my father who provided me with a role model for engineering excellence, and to my mother who in so many ways took an active part in my education. The encouragement and support never stopped, with the possible exception of the time Mom tried to discourage the purchase of my first computer. In retrospect, she must have understood its architectural shortcomings. After all, it wasn't a parallel processor.

I am grateful beyond words for the love, concern, encouragement, and support given me by my wife Susan and my sons Robbie and Peter.

Most of all, I thank my Lord who made the path clear and who guided each step.

**PARALLEL MACHINES: PARALLEL
MACHINE LANGUAGES**

**The Emergence of Hybrid Dataflow
Computer Architectures**

Chapter One

The Problem Domain

This text considers the space of architectures which fit the description of scalable, general purpose parallel computers. The term PARALLEL COMPUTER denotes a collection of computing resources, specifically, some number of identical, asynchronously operating processors, some number of identical memory units, and some means for intercommunication, assembled for the purpose of cooperating on the solution of problems[1]. Such problems are decomposed into communicating parts which are mapped onto the processors. GENERAL PURPOSE means simply that such computers can exploit parallelism, when present, in any program, without appealing to some specific attribute unique to some specific problem domain. SCALABILITY implies that, given sufficient program parallelism, adding hardware resources will result in higher performance without requiring program alteration. The scaling range is assumed to be from a single processor up to a thousand processors[2]. Parallelism significantly beyond this limit demands yet another change in viewpoint for both machines and languages.

In this Chapter, the groundwork is laid for understanding the issues of parallel machine architecture. The starting point, in Section 1.1, is a representation for parallel programs which abstracts away underlying architectures yet is below the level of programming languages. Such a representation permits fairly concrete reasoning about the features demanded of a parallel machine from the programming perspective with-

---

[1]In the remainder of this text, the term PARALLEL MACHINE will refer to such a scalable, general purpose parallel computer. Contrast this definition with that of a MULTIPROCESSOR: a multiple-processor computer used to exploit parallelism between disparate processes rather than the parallelism within one process.

[2]By Bell's metric [11], this is an architectural dynamic range of 30 dB.

out unduly binding the arguments to a particular language or set of languages. Following this, the fundamental nature of latency and synchronization in a parallel machine is exposed in Section 1.2. With a basic understanding of how programs are represented, and with the fundamental issues of parallel machines well in hand, economic metrics which reflect the cost of parallelism are developed in Section 1.3. These measures will, throughout the text, guide the development of a new architecture both in analyzing existing approaches and in choosing between new alternatives.

1.1 ABSTRACT PROGRAM REPRESENTATION

Throughout this text, architectural features are motivated on the basis of programming requirements. While it is not the purpose here to analyze high level programming languages, it is relevant to have some means of representing programs which captures the essence of parallel program expression. Such a representation should reflect all and only the sequentializing constraints of programs without imposing further linguistic or, worse yet, machine-specific constraints.

The DATAFLOW PROGRAM GRAPH (DFPG) [56] is a powerful and elegant intermediate representation for programs which meets these requirements. DFPG's are largely architecture independent and have precise semantics. In this Section, the structure of DFPG's is summarized through the use of an example. As part of the example, code fragments from the Id programming language [9] are used to specify the programs to be represented as DFPG's. It should be understood that the focus here is on the graphs, not Id, and that it is indeed possible to translate programs in other languages into DFPG's.

The DFPG programming model is made up of a set of rules for composing, or building, well-formed graphs along with an interpretation rule which defines the operational semantics of a program expressed as a DFPG. This is based on the classic dataflow model [22], but it should be understood that the model, not the dataflow embodiment, is assumed here. The reader must accept on faith that these two are separable; in other words, that the dataflow style of expressing programs does not restrict the implementation to dataflow machines. Intuitively, the value is that expressing programs as fine-grained parallel graphs at some point during program compilation admits more forms of analysis than do other, more coarse-grained representations.

Traub [56] defines DFPG's as follows:

> The program graph is composed of a collection of instructions, each with an opcode that identifies its function, and some number of inputs and outputs. A directed arc connecting an output to an input allows a piece of data called a token to flow along that arc. For convenience, we will assume that any particular output may be connected to an arbitrary number of inputs (but not the reverse); the token emitted by an output is copied and sent to all inputs to which the output is connected.

It is presumed that an arc represents a static data dependence, and that transitive static dependence (C depends on B which depends on A, therefore, C depends on A) is meaningful but not directly expressed as an additional arc. Lack of such dependence between instructions, then, implies that the instructions are candidates for parallel execution. Certain classes of instructions give rise to a notion of DYNAMIC DEPENDENCE, *i.e.*, one which cannot be predicted by static analysis of the program. These instructions and dependences will be described and treated in depth in a later Section.

Operationally, instructions are considered as executable when and only when their firing rule is satisfied. The FIRING RULE is a predicate on the presence or absence of tokens at the instruction's inputs. A token is said to be present on a given input of a given instruction if and only if a token has been placed on the corresponding arc. Firing, or executing, an instruction consumes tokens on input arcs and produces side effects and/or tokens which are placed on output arcs.

The firing rule as implied by the graph is a necessary, but not sufficient, pre-condition to actual instruction execution. Additional constraints may be imposed by a specific architecture. Moreover, the means of implementing the firing rule is not presumed but is an architectural degree of freedom. One extreme is EXPLICIT SCHEDULING wherein the architecture literally implements the detection of token presence and the satisfaction of firing constraints at program execution time. The other extreme is IMPLICIT SCHEDULING wherein the firing rules are, in some sense, inherent in the way the machine code is expressed. Explicit scheduling is dynamic, while implicit scheduling is static.

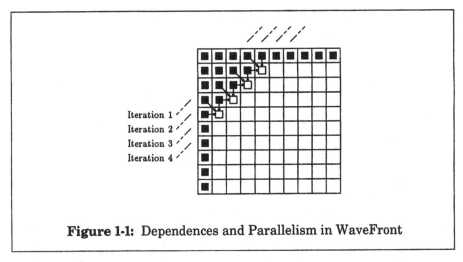

Figure 1-1: Dependences and Parallelism in WaveFront

The WaveFront Example

Presented below is a simple program called WaveFront which will be used throughout this text. It takes as input an initialization vector of length *n*. The program allocates a matrix of dimension *n×n*, fills in the first row and first column from corresponding elements of the initialization vector, then proceeds to compute the remaining elements as follows: each empty element's value is the average of three near-neighbor values — the north, west, and northwest.

```
def wavefront edge_vector =
  {l,u = 1d_bounds edge_vector;
   m    = matrix ((l,u),(l,u));
   m[l,l] = edge_vector[l];
   {for i from l+1 to u do
      m[l,i] = edge_vector[i];
      m[i,l] = edge_vector[i];};
   {for i from l+1 to u do
      {for j from l+1 to u do
         m[i,j] = (m[i-1,j] + m[i,j-1] +
                   m[i-1,j-1]) / 3;}}
   in
     m};
```

After having filled in the first row and first column, the computation logically proceeds as shown in Figure 1-1, with all unfilled cells along any one diagonal being candidates for parallel execution.

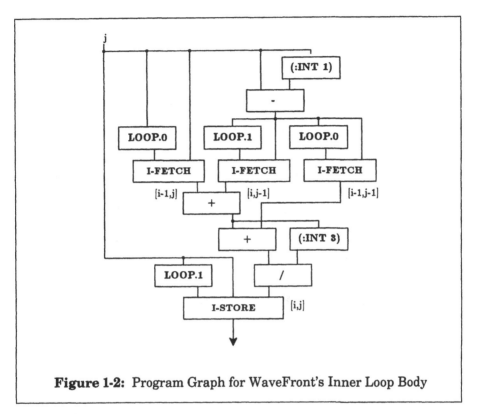

Figure 1-2: Program Graph for WaveFront's Inner Loop Body

Expressions

In order to understand the instructions that make up a DFPG, the types of data which traverse the arcs, and the firing rules, consider the doubly-nested inner loop of WaveFront.

Figure 1-2 shows the DFPG for the body of the inner loop. Given the value of j, three elements are fetched from the matrix, they are arithmetically averaged, and the result is stored into the matrix. The matrix is represented as a column-vector of I-Structure descriptors[3] for the rows.

---

[3]I-Structures and their semantics are described in Section 2.2. For the sake of this discussion, I-Structures may be viewed as memory-bound one dimensional arrays, the elements of which may be read and written with the operations I-FETCH and I-STORE. These instructions are similar to traditional LOAD and STORE but also perform synchronization operations. References to I-Structures are made with I-Structure descriptors which may be thought of as pointers.

Fetching the i,j^{th} element, then, requires first fetching the ith I-Structure descriptor from the column-vector and then fetching the jth element. Because of the addressing pattern implicit in the expression, the graph for the body of the inner loop requires the I-Structure descriptor of both the ith and $i-1^{st}$ rows. Furthermore, because these descriptors are invariant across iterations, they appear as constants, represented by **LOOP-CONSTANT** instructions:

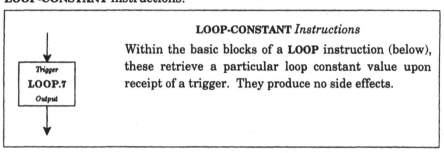

LOOP-CONSTANT *Instructions*

Within the basic blocks of a **LOOP** instruction (below), these retrieve a particular loop constant value upon receipt of a trigger. They produce no side effects.

The first loop constant (**LOOP.0**) is the I-Structure descriptor for the $i-1^{st}$ row of matrix M. The second loop constant (**LOOP.1**) is the I-Structure descriptor for the ith row. These descriptors are "produced" when the trigger, *i.e.*, the loop index, becomes available.

Literal constants are also explicitly represented in the program graph:

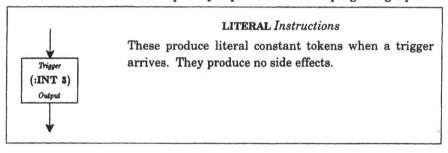

LITERAL *Instructions*

These produce literal constant tokens when a trigger arrives. They produce no side effects.

Thus, loop constant and literal inputs to a graph are not represented as tokens until an appropriate constant instruction generates them. In the case of the WaveFront graph, no tokens are present until the token carrying the value of j arrives.

Arithmetic and logical operations are represented in the graph by monadic and dyadic instructions, as appropriate.

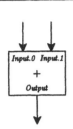

MONADIC/DYADIC *Instructions*

These include the usual spectrum of arithmetic and logical operations. These instructions fire only when all input tokens are present, produce an output token, and have no side effects. A number of special monadic instructions extract fields from structured tokens (to be described) and have no side effects.

In the example graph, it is now easy to see how the indices for the three I-Structure references are expressed: addressing of the ith and $i-1^{st}$ rows is done by selecting the appropriate I-Structure descriptor. In this case, since the descriptors were loop invariants, this means simply using the right loop constant. Addressing of the particular element in the row is done via the **I-FETCH** instruction and the appropriately-calculated index.

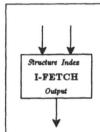

I-FETCH *Instructions*

Given a token carrying an I-Structure descriptor and a token carrying a slot offset, these instructions fire and produce a token which is the value of the given slot of the given structure.

Thus, the three **I-FETCH** instructions will fetch, respectively, elements $i-1,j$, $i,j-1$, and $i-1,j-1$. These values are averaged, and the result is stored in element i,j.

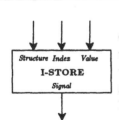

I-STORE *Instructions*

Given a token carrying an I-Structure descriptor, a token carrying a slot offset, and a token carrying a value, these instructions fire, write the value into the given slot of the given I-Structure (a side-effect), and produce a signal token.

The sole explicit output of this expression is the signal emanating from this **I-STORE** instruction.

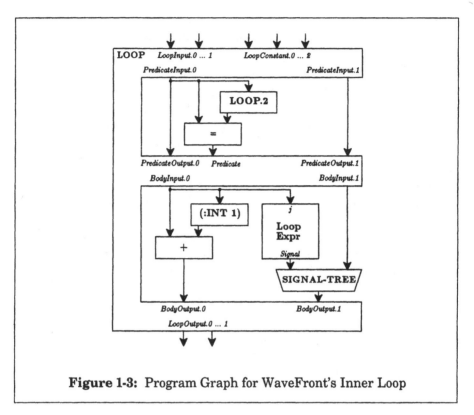

Figure 1-3: Program Graph for WaveFront's Inner Loop

Loops

Looping, using the given expression as a body, is represented with a different class of program graph instruction called **LOOP** (Figure 1-3). **LOOP** is an abstraction of an instruction schema; Traub [56] refers to such an abstraction as an ENCAPSULATOR: an instruction which, in addition to an exterior surface, has interior surfaces which enclose other program graph instructions. Sets of instructions so enclosed by a given input/output surface pair are called BASIC BLOCKS.

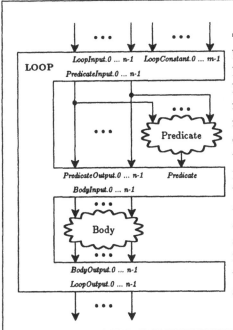

LOOP *Encapsulators*

These enclose a *Predicate* basic block and a *Body* basic block, and hide the details of loop invocation, loop constant management, bounding, and recycling of per-iteration resources. Upon arrival of the loop constant tokens and any loop input tokens, the predicate is evaluated, producing a boolean token. If TRUE, the loop body is executed, producing a new set of loop variables which are recirculated to the predicate associated with the *next* iteration. If FALSE, the loop variables are routed to the output of the **LOOP** encapsulator.

In the Figure, the predicate consists of a relational instruction which compares the loop index *j* with the loop limit (available as the third loop constant, **LOOP.2**). The body consists of the entire graph of Figure 1-2, instructions to increment the loop index, and a **SIGNAL-TREE** instruction which tests for termination of the iteration.

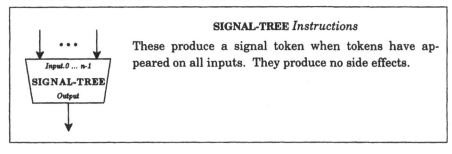

SIGNAL-TREE *Instructions*

These produce a signal token when tokens have appeared on all inputs. They produce no side effects.

At this point, the reader should have a basic understanding of the components which make up a DFPG, and some understanding of what such graphs mean. Rules for constructing DFPG's from high level languages

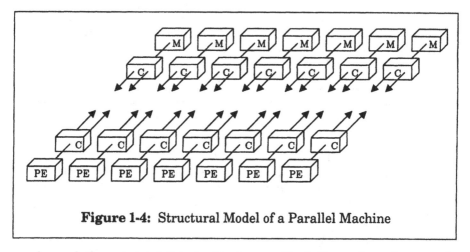

Figure 1-4: Structural Model of a Parallel Machine

are beyond the scope of this text. An excellent discussion of one such translation mechanism is given in [56]. In subsequent Chapters, other instructions, such as **IF**, will be presented as the need arises.

Data Types

Tokens may represent scalar values or pointers. Scalars may be integers, floating point numbers, booleans, or symbols. Pointers include I-Structure descriptors (references to **CONS** cells [44], tuples, strings, vectors, structures, or arrays) and closure descriptors. This set of data types is closed under the operations defined by the DFPG instruction set.

1.2 TWO FUNDAMENTAL ISSUES

Latency and synchronization are fundamental issues which must be faced by all architects of parallel machines. These issues are discussed in [8] and are summarized here. A parallel machine is, by definition, a collection of computing resources. Because the processors and memories in the collection occupy physical space, there will necessarily be limitations on the time to communicate between them. The organization of a parallel machine, therefore, gives rise to latency. Similarly, by definition, parallel machines imply the cooperation of processors on the solution of a single problem. Therefore, problems must be logically decomposed into communicating fragments, implying the need for some sort of time-coordination, or synchronization. These issues are examined in depth in the following Sections.

Latency: The First Fundamental Issue

The organization of any parallel machine can be thought of as an interconnection of the following three types of modules (see Figure 1-4):

1. COMMUNICATION ELEMENTs (C's): Modules which transport data. Each nontrivial communication element has at least three communication ports. Communication elements neither originate nor receive synchronizing signals, instructions, or data; rather, they retransmit such information when received on one of the communication ports to one or more of the other communication ports. Communication elements are characterized by the rate of transmission, the time taken per transmission, and the constraints imposed by one transmission on others, *e.g.*, blocking. The maximum amount of data that may be conveyed on a communication port per unit time is fixed.

2. PROCESSING ELEMENTs (PE's): Modules which perform arithmetic and logical operations on data. Each processing element has a single communication port. PE's interact with other PE's by sending messages, issuing interrupts or sending and receiving synchronizing signals through shared memory. PE's interact with memory elements by issuing **LOAD** and **STORE** instructions modified as necessary with atomicity constraints. PE's are characterized by the rate at which they can process instructions.

3. MEMORY ELEMENTs (M's): Modules which store data. Each memory element has a single communication port. Memory elements respond to requests issued by the PE's by returning data through the communication port, and are characterized by their total capacity and the rate at which they respond to these requests[4].

For a real parallel machine, any computation running on it is constrained to occupy nonzero volume, and any communication within that volume is subject to speed-of-light limits. Given this physical distribution in space, the concept of latency is of great significance.

---

[4]In many traditional designs, the memory subsystem can be simply modeled by one of these M elements. Interleaved memory subsystems are modeled as a collection of M's and C's. Memory subsystems which incorporate processing capability can be modeled with PE's, M's, and C's.

Definition 1-1: LATENCY is the time which elapses between making a request and receiving the associated response. LATENCY COST is the useful processing time, typically measured in machine cycles, which is lost due to waiting, or idling, in the presence of latency.

The structural model implies that a PE in a parallel machine faces larger latency in memory references than a serial machine (uniprocessor) does because of the transit time in the communication network between PE's and the memories. This argument is quite independent of notions of locality and network topology. Latency can, but does not always, incur cost.

Consider the model that either all memory modules in a multiprocessor form one global address space out of which any processor can read any word, or a model in which processors communicate directly with one another via messages, the memories being strictly local to processors. Either model demonstrates that latency means much more than simply delay, *to wit*:

- **Latency is Variable:** The time to fetch an operand / communicate a value in a message may not be constant because some memories / processors may be closer than others in the physical organization of the machine (locality).

- **Latency Cannot be Bounded:** No useful bound on the worst case time to fetch / send a value may be possible at machine design time because of the scalability assumption.

- **Chaos Arises out of Order:** If a processor were to issue several (pipelined) requests to different remote memory modules / processors in a given order, the responses could arrive in a different order.

Synchronization: The Second Fundamental Issue

In order to effect parallel computation, the description of a program must be broken into many small fragments. Such decomposition may be done manually or automatically, *e.g.*, by some algorithm which partitions DFPG's. The static entities into which a program is decomposed are called scheduling quanta, for they are the largest units within which the decomposing agent, human or algorithm, has direct scheduling control, and the smallest units which the run-time system can manipulate. SQ's may be as small as a single instruction or as large as an entire procedure.

Definition 1-2: A SCHEDULING QUANTUM (SQ) is a nonempty total ordering of machine instructions along with some un-
ambiguous rule for interpreting, or executing, them.

In operation, an SQ is instantiated by associating with it some private execution state. Instantiated SQ's are represented by objects called continuations which denote both the static SQ and the dynamic invocation
state.

Definition 1-3: A CONTINUATION is a dynamic (run-time) object
which denotes an instance of an SQ, that is, its instruction text
plus its instance-specific state.

A continuation[5] is to an SQ what a process is to a procedure. At run time
there may be many instantiations of a given SQ, each represented by a
distinct continuation. Continuations are created dynamically during a
computation and die after having produced and consumed data. Continuations are mapped onto processors and operate in mutual asynchrony.
Because decomposing a program leads to the issue of coordination, the
concept of synchronization is of concern.

Definition 1-4: SYNCHRONIZATION is the time-coordination of
the continuations within a computation. SYNCHRONIZATION
COST is the useful processing time, typically measured in
machine cycles, which is lost due to the providing of time-
coordination.

Synchronization cost is a much more elusive concept than latency cost. In
order to understand it more fully, the basic classes of synchronization
primitives are analyzed, the underlying mechanisms they mandate are
identified, and the cost of providing these mechanisms is described. Consider these examples of synchronization metaphors:

1. FORK / JOIN PARALLELISM: A continuation is created as a
   result of a **FORK** operation, and can run concurrently with the
   creating continuation until encountering a **JOIN** operation.
   The **JOIN** enforces synchronization and ultimately results in
   the termination of the forked continuation.

2. PRODUCER-CONSUMER PARALLELISM: Given two extant con-

---

[5]Occasionally, the term *context* is used for "continuation" when speaking of switching
or management in that it is a more natural term for the same concept.

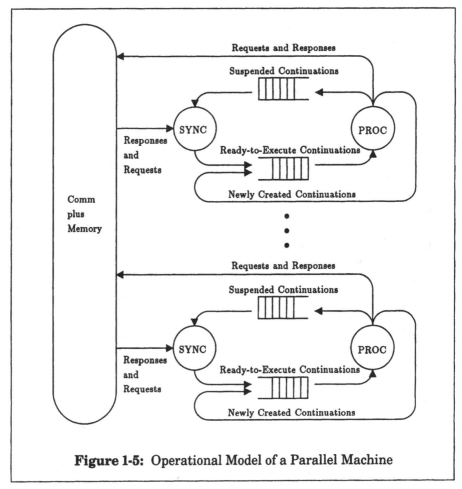

Figure 1-5: Operational Model of a Parallel Machine

tinuations, one produces a data structure which is consumed by the other. If producer and consumer are executed in parallel, element-by-element coordination is needed to avoid the *read-before-write* race.

3. MUTUAL EXCLUSION: Extant continuations share some serially reusable resource, and means must be provided to guarantee that only one continuation at a time may have access to it. Because the behavior depends on the time-ordering of requests, non-determinism is implied.

All such synchronization mechanisms involve identification of the participants (continuations), identification of a meeting ground, testing for satisfaction of some synchronization constraint, and blocking in the event that the synchronization constraint is not satisfied. The MEETING GROUND is represented by some unique name known to the participants along with at least one bit's worth of information — the encoding of an EVENT. If the bit is not set, it is said that the event is pending. If the bit is set, it is said that the event has occurred. Operationally, a synchronization operation involves testing to see if an event has occurred and then taking one of two alternative actions based on the result of the test. If an event has occurred, the computation may proceed normally. If it has not, some other action must take place which serves to block the normal computation from proceeding. This may have the form of an enforced busy-waiting for the event which inevitably wastes computing resources. Alternatively, the continuation making the synchronization test can be put aside to have the test tried again at a later time. Such putting aside is called CONTEXT SWITCHing in which the continuation's private state is evacuated from the PE and, optionally, another continuation's state is installed. Often, the terms ROLLING OUT and ROLLING IN are used to describe this process.

Participants may be viewed as being in one of the following states at any given time: *ready-to-execute*, *executing*, or *suspended*, with state transitions happening at synchronization, scheduling, and context switching points, respectively (see Figure 1-5).

With this framework it is now possible to consider synchronization cost. The most obvious costs are those associated with testing for the occurrence of an event and those related to conditional blocking. Testing cost is incurred once for each test. A busy-waiting scheme will accrue this cost over time, depending on the frequency of the testing. Conditional blocking cost may be zero in the case that the first test succeeds. It may be finite in the case that a failed test incurs the cost of a one-time evacuation of the continuation. In the worst case, it may be unbounded in a busy-waiting scheme.

There are numerous subtle issues in accounting for the remaining synchronization costs. Because participants and events are named, synchronization cost must also include the costs of generating, matching and reusing the names. It may not be easy to identify the instructions executed for this purpose. Nevertheless, such instructions represent over-head because they would not be present if the program were written and compiled to execute on a uniprocessor.

Another subtle issue has to do with the accounting for intra-continuation synchronization. Because most high performance computers overlap the execution of instructions belonging to one continuation, techniques used for synchronization of instructions within the continuation, *e.g.*, because of instruction prefetch delays at a branch point, are often quite different from techniques for inter-continuation synchronization. In these cases, busy-waiting in the form of instruction dispatcher interlock or the execution of compiled-in NOP instructions is usually safer and cheaper than context switching. This is done under the assumption that the idle time will be strictly less than the time to switch contexts. These lost cycles are as much a synchronization cost as are those associated with context switching.

More subtle yet is the cost which arises when the synchronization name space is small (as it usually is in schemes employing registers or interrupt levels as the meeting places). SYNCHRONIZATION NAME SPACE implies a coupling of three necessarily efficient attributes of an architecture: the ability to name participants, the ability to name meeting places, and the ability to enforce synchronizing behavior (*e.g.*, blocking). In this sense, registers with reservation bits plus an instruction dispatcher which tests the bits *almost* represents a synchronization name space, as long as one is willing to accept busy-waiting. Without busy-waiting, context switching, and the associated naming of the switched continuations, is essential. Traditional semaphores in main memory do not represent a synchronization name space. While the name of the meeting place, an address, can be generated cheaply, the enforcing of synchronizing behavior if done in software is expensive. Multiple hardware-maintained contexts coupled with synchronizing registers does represent a synchronization name space, albeit a small one. The issue of a *small* synchronization name space is that names themselves (each context has a unique name, typically tied to some hardware entity; each register also has a unique name) are serially reusable resources which must be managed. Often this management is done at compile time, and the cost takes the elusive form of a restricted number of simultaneously pending synchronization events. This translates into an artificially constrained degree of parallelism.

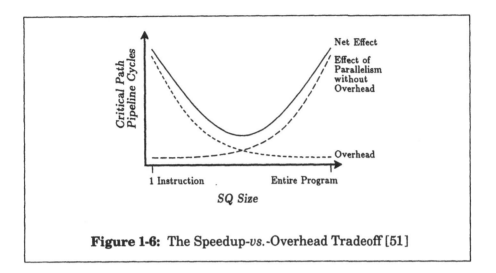

Figure 1-6: The Speedup-*vs.*-Overhead Tradeoff [51]

In summary, synchronization incurs cost, but the total cost is a function of the efficiency of the mechanisms and the degree to which synchronization is used. Unfortunately, in models where the cost is much more than the cost of, say, an arithmetic instruction, these two factors (efficiency and degree of use) are seldom independent. The efficiency function may be non-linear (*e.g.*, the cost of generating and using another synchronization name may be zero until some hardware-specific limit is reached — the cost then goes off the scale).

1.3 THE COST OF PARALLELISM

Given that latency and synchronization are fundamental to parallel machines, and given that each can result in tangible costs, what can be said about the fundamental costs of parallel computation? One very clear measure of the cost of parallel execution is the CRITICAL PATH LENGTH of the compiled program in an idealized, non-resource constrained environment. It is measured in time units by simulation or by analytical means and then normalized to some generally-accepted universal unit such as pipeline cycles or RISC-style instructions. The critical path length gives a lower bound on the execution time for a given compiled program. It reflects the constraints of the abstract architecture, but ignores constraints of particular machine configurations, *e.g.*, the number of processors.

Given a proper definition of latency and synchronization costs for a particular architecture, it is an interesting, if disconcerting, fact that an optimal cost and therefore an optimal level of parallelism is implied for any given program, beyond which the program will actually run slower if an attempt is made to exploit more parallelism. This speedup-*vs.*-overhead tradeoff provided the motivation for Sarkar's optimization problem [51] wherein the division of an abstract program specification into SQ's is driven by an architecture-specific economic model (Figure 1-6). As the size of each SQ becomes smaller, the fixed overhead associated with enabling, scheduling, and otherwise synchronizing it very quickly dominates the execution time. At one extreme, the SQ size is the entire program *i.e.*, a single SQ. Clearly, no parallelism can be exploited when there is but a single locus of control, but the overhead cost is indeed minimized. At the other extreme, SQ size is at a minimum and parallelism can be exploited maximally. However, the overhead cost dominates the useful computation. It is only somewhere in between that the architecture-specific overhead costs balance the uncovered parallelism — a kind of HALF-POWER POINT for the architecture. This says that for a fixed architecture, there is a minimum SQ size below which programs will take longer to execute. One might call this *architecture-directed partitioning*.

In this text we consider the flip side of the issue, specifically, *partitioning-directed architecture*. In terms of Figure 1-6, this means taking the architecture, and therefore the overhead curve, as a variable. Such architectures seek to mitigate the costs of latency and synchronization (overhead) both by providing specific hardware support for explicit synchronization and by offering the means in the programming model whereby the costs can be explicitly managed. This management takes the form of a controllable tradeoff between explicit and implicit instruction scheduling. Under an EXPLICIT SCHEDULING discipline, instruction n can be scheduled at any time t only if it is known that instruction $n-1$ has *completed* its execution at some time $t' < t$. Under the IMPLICIT SCHEDULING discipline, instruction n can be scheduled at any time t only if it is known that instruction $n-1$ has been *scheduled* to execute at some time $t' < t$. This distinction becomes important in PIPELINEd machines wherein one instruction may enter the PE at each cycle but where the time to completely execute a single instruction takes $p > 1$ cycles[6]. It is

---

[6]The value p is frequently called the PIPELINE DEPTH.

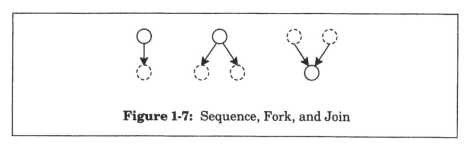

Figure 1-7: Sequence, Fork, and Join

nearly a foregone conclusion today that any high performance PE will be pipelined.

In the next Sections, two simple example graphs are analyzed to motivate an understanding of the implicit / explicit tradeoff.

Assumptions

In the graphs to be analyzed, it is assumed that the in-degree of each instruction is either one or two, that each instruction has exactly one output, and that the out-degree of this output is either one or two[7]. The analysis hinges on assessing the costs of the three forms of low-level program graph instructions shown in Figure 1-7. These instructions will have machine-specific realizations and associated costs which make the differences more apparent. Specifically, instructions with out-degree of two imply **FORK**ing (creation of parallel work), and instructions with an in-degree of two imply **JOIN**ing (synchronization). Call the total execution time of a **FORK** instruction C_f and the total execution time of a **JOIN** instruction C_j. These times are normalized to the execution time of a non-forking, non-joining instruction.

Analysis

Consider the following two examples (Figure 1-8). In the first, the graph to be executed is a simple linear sequence of instructions. In the second, a binary tree of fork operations is followed by an inverted tree of join operations. These examples are chosen not purely for their simplicity: the first is the limiting case of sequentiality, and the second is the limiting case of

---

[7]These assumptions are consistent with the semantics of low-level instructions on a variety of existing machines. Conceptual instructions which violate these constraints (*e.g.*, more inputs, fan-out greater than two) can typically be re-written into interconnections of simpler instructions which adhere to the constraints.

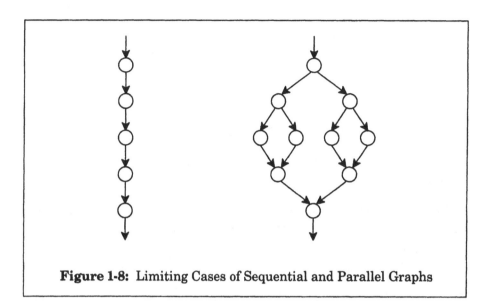

Figure 1-8: Limiting Cases of Sequential and Parallel Graphs

parallelism based on the above assumptions plus single graph input and single graph output. In execution, it is interesting to count the number of pipeline beats required for execution as a function of the number of instructions n.

Analysis of the sequential case is conceptually straightforward. Given an initial value, instructions can be scheduled for execution one after the other, with intermediate values being passed from instruction to instruction. It is easy to see that n instructions, under implicit scheduling, will take $n+p-1$ cycles to complete. Under explicit scheduling, however, the same sequential chain will take $n \times p$ cycles to complete.

In the parallel case, the analysis is slightly more complex. Because a binary tree with k leaves has $k-1$ non-leaf nodes, it follows that

$$n = 3k - 2 \qquad\qquad [1]$$

For $n \gg 1$, $k \approx \frac{n}{3}$. That is, for large programs, fully one third of the instructions will be **FORK**s, one third will be **JOIN**s, and one third will be normal instructions. Assume a program which is large relative to the parallel processor on which it will be executed, *i.e.*, $n \gg PE's$. Under either explicit or implicit scheduling, all PE's can be kept busy on every cycle, save a

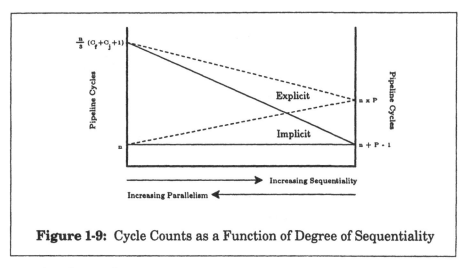

Figure 1-9: Cycle Counts as a Function of Degree of Sequentiality

vanishingly small fraction of time at program start-up and termination (due to spreading and coalescing). In either case, the execution time will be

$$\frac{n}{3}(C_f + C_j + 1) \qquad [2]$$

Presume that, in the best case, $C_f = C_j = 1$. What this implies for architectures is simply this: handling programs or parts of programs with low-degree parallelism requires either an implicit instruction scheduling mechanism or a very shallow pipeline, while handling programs or parts of programs with high-degree parallelism requires low cost creation of parallel work (spawning of continuations) and low cost synchronization. The tradeoff, as a function of degree of parallelism (or sequentiality, depending on one's point of view), is depicted in Figure 1-9.

1.4 SUMMARY

This chapter has defined the domain of interest as scalable, general purpose parallel computing. Within this domain, programs may be represented in a variety of ways which expose more or less of the available parallelism. One particularly suitable intermediate representation, below the level of textual languages but above the level of machine code, is the Dataflow Program Graph. This form represents only essential data dependences and has the property that wherever there is no interdependence between instructions, parallelism is implied.

Further, it has been argued that latency and synchronization are fundamental issues within the domain of scalable, general purpose parallel computation. Latency arises from the physical distribution in space of the modules which make up a parallel computer. The need for synchronization arises when one seeks to map a single computation over multiple, asynchronously operating processors.

Because of the fundamental issues, there is a cost associated with running a program in parallel. Moreover, there are hard limits imposed by any specific architecture on the degree to which one may exploit decomposing an application for parallel execution. It is the goal of parallel machine architects to push back these limits by addressing the fundamental issues.

The next chapter considers previous architectural attempts within the domain of parallel machines. This retrospective is presented in the light of the foregoing discussion.

Chapter Two

The Importance of

Processor Architecture

Current-day multiprocessors represent the general belief that processor architecture is of little importance in designing parallel machines. In this Chapter, the fallacy of this assumption will be demonstrated on the basis of the two fundamental issue of latency and synchronization. The argument is based on the following observations:

1. Physical parallelism implies latency for both processor-to-memory and processor-to-processor communications.

2. Latency scales up with the number of processors.

3. Traditional processors employing simple von Neumann style instruction scheduling will idle when executing any instruction which incurs this latency.

4. Attempting to go beyond this limit implies the need for efficient, hardware-level synchronization means.

5. Based on the cost of using such hardware, only certain types of parallelism can be exploited efficiently.

In Section 2.1, the shortcomings of von Neumann architecture are explored in more detail. The traditional methods used to reduce the effect of memory latency in von Neumann computers are examined, and their limitations are discussed. A similar discussion of synchronization methods is presented. Section 2.2 looks critically at dataflow architecture and attempts to articulate its strengths and weaknesses. Section 2.3 seeks to compare the two architectures and the types of parallelism which can be exploited. On the negative side, this comparison highlights the inflexibility of the von Neumann approach and shows the inefficiency of the dataflow approach. From a positivist's view, the example focuses attention on efficient mechanisms for implicit and explicit synchronization which one would like to combine in a new architecture.

2.1 VON NEUMANN ARCHITECTURES

Various mechanisms have been invented to deal with latency and synchronization costs for von Neumann uniprocessor architectures. Here, these are analyzed and are shown to be ineffective when used in a parallel von Neumann machine.

Tolerating Latency

A variety of strategies have been tried throughout the history of computer architecture in an effort to reduce the effect of memory latency on computation time. All of these seek to uncouple memory reference performance from processor performance either by migrating essential data to reside within the processor proper (registers, data caches) and/or by hiding memory latency behind an otherwise occupied processor (instruction prefetching, instruction caches, pipelining, LOAD/STORE organization). These solutions to latency problems share the interesting property that, if applied without modification to a parallel machine, they potentially introduce synchronization problems.

Increasing the Processor State. In the earliest computers, such as ED-SAC, the processor state consisted solely of an accumulator, a quotient register, and a program counter. Memories were relatively slow compared to the processors, and thus, the time to fetch an instruction and its operands completely dominated the instruction cycle time; arithmetic performance was incidental.

By investing in some additional high-speed storage, *e.g.*, multiple accumulators, a new game was possible: a computation could be organized to load these accumulators from memory, to perform some computation using only the accumulators, and to store the final results. The increase in processor state meant that, at least for the accumulator-only instructions, instruction execution time could be made independent of the long-latency memory. However, the enlarged processor state still did not help reduce the time lost during memory references and, consequently, did not contribute to an overall reduction in cycle time. Perhaps the most significant effect of increased state was the introduction of index registers which eliminated the need for self-modifying code, bringing an attendant reduction in the total number of instructions executed.

Instruction Pre-fetching. The time lost to instruction fetching can be totally hidden, and the cycle time thereby improved, if fetching is done during the execution phase of the previous instruction (PRE-FETCHING). If instructions and data are kept in separate memories, it is similarly possible to overlap some amount of operand fetching as well (The IBM STRETCH [13] and Univac LARC [24] represent two of the earliest attempts at implementing this idea).

Instruction pre-fetching works well only when the execution of instruction i does not have any effect on either the choice of instructions to fetch (as in the case of **BRANCH**) or the content of the fetched instruction (self-modifying code) for instructions $i+1$, $i+2$, ..., $i+k$. The latter case is usually handled by simply outlawing it. However, effective overlapped execution in the presence of **BRANCH** instructions has remained a problem. Techniques such as pre-fetching both **BRANCH** targets have shown little performance/cost benefits. However, the microprogramming trick of delayed **BRANCH** instructions has been incorporated, with success, in **LOAD/STORE** architectures. The idea is to delay the effect of a **BRANCH** by one instruction. Thus, the instruction at $i+1$ following a **BRANCH** instruction at i is always executed regardless of which way the **BRANCH** at i goes. One can always follow a **BRANCH** instruction with a **NOP** instruction to get the old effect. However, experience has shown that seventy percent of the time a useful instruction can be put in that position.

Operand pre-fetching is subject to similar dependence constraints from previously issued instructions. In sequential code, it is quite common that an operand for instruction i is the result of instruction $i-1$. It is necessary to synchronize these two instructions so as to guarantee that instruction i gets the correct value. One method, called BYPASSING, is to force the operand prefetch hardware to ignore the value it would have normally fetched and to substitute the value to be produced by instruction $i-1$ when this kind of dependence is detected. A variant on this scheme is to delay the fetching of operands for instruction i until instruction $i-1$ has stored its result. This technique is referred to as INTERLOCKING. The attendant delay, or idle time, is commonly called a BUBBLE.

Because overlap is not applicable to all cases of all instructions, an architect must pay the price of increased complexity in terms of synchronization hardware to detect and deal with the special cases, or he must forego these optimizations.

Instruction Buffers, Operand Caches and Pipelined Execution.
The time to fetch instructions can be further reduced by providing a fast instruction buffer, further increasing the processor state. In machines such as the CDC 6600 [54] and the Cray-1 [50], the instruction buffer is automatically loaded with n instructions in the neighborhood of a referenced instruction whenever the referenced instruction is found to be missing. Similarly, operand fetching can be optimized by providing operand caches which prefetch and store data values which are in the neighborhood of a referenced datum. Both of these techniques rely on locality: because of sequential instruction interpretation, given the execution of instruction i, the next instruction to be executed will be, with very high probability, $i+1$. Transitivity further implies the need for $i+2$, $i+3$, and so on. The probability density function (PDF) of likely successor instructions, given i, is strongly centered about i as opposed to being uniformly distributed. Therefore, there is economic value in pre-fetching program text in the neighborhood of a referenced instruction from a slow storage (main memory) into a higher speed buffer in the processor. If many such instructions can be pre-fetched with a single memory reference, the total number of references can be reduced, and the memory access time will become more a function of buffer speed. If the PDF of instructions can be used to infer a similar PDF for the associated operands, operand caches can magnify the main memory's apparent speed for data as well. This class of locality, called SPATIAL LOCALITY, relates characteristics of one fetch operation with the characteristics of other fetch instructions. In subsequent Chapters, the kindred concept of TEMPORAL LOCALITY will be exploited. This relates characteristics of one store operation with the characteristics of other fetch instructions (*i.e.*, that a value, once produced, will likely be consumed shortly thereafter).

As each stage of instruction processing is optimized, the natural generalization is to organize the processor as a PIPELINE, dividing the total instruction execution task into a number of equivalently-sized subtasks, *e.g.*, fetching the instruction from the instruction cache in the first stage, decoding it in the second stage, fetching the operands from the

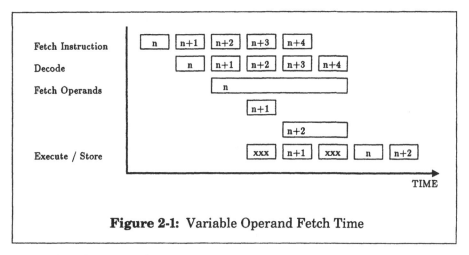

Figure 2-1: Variable Operand Fetch Time

operand cache in the third stage, and so on. The hope is to be able to dispatch instructions with a periodicity (called the pipeline STEP or BEAT) equal to the time taken by the slowest pipeline stage, rather than the time taken by the sum of the stages.

Designing a well-balanced pipeline requires that the time taken by various pipeline stages be more or less equal, and that the "things", *i.e.*, instructions, entering the pipe be independent of each other. Obviously, instructions of a program cannot be totally independent except in certain degenerate cases. Instructions in a pipe are usually related in one of two ways: Instruction *n* produces data needed by instruction *n+k*, or only the complete execution of instruction *n* determines the next instruction to be executed (the aforementioned **BRANCH** problem).

Limitations on hardware resources can also cause instructions to interfere with one another. Consider the case wherein both instructions *n* and *n+1* require an adder, but there is only one of these in the machine. Obviously, one of the instructions must be deferred until the other is complete. A pipelined machine must be able to prevent a new instruction from entering the pipeline temporarily when there is a possibility of interference with the instructions already in the pipe. Detecting and quickly resolving these hazards is very difficult with ordinary instruction sets, *e.g.*, IBM System/370, DEC VAX, or Motorola 680x0, due to their complexity.

A major complication in pipelining complex instructions occurs when the stage time is not strictly bounded, *e.g.*, when memory / communication latency is involved. Even more troublesome is the possibility that responses to such long-latency operations may arrive out-of-order, as in Figure 2-1, necessitating some form of synchronization.

LOAD/STORE Architectures. A variety of instruction sets, pioneered in the 1960s [54], divides instructions into two disjoint classes. In one class are instructions which move data unchanged between memory and high speed registers. In the other class are instructions which operate on data in the registers. Instructions of the second class cannot access the memory. This rigid distinction simplifies instruction scheduling. For each instruction, it is trivial to see if a memory reference will be necessary or not. Moreover, the memory system and the ALU may be viewed as parallel, noninteracting pipelines. An instruction dispatches exactly one unit of work to either one pipe or the other, but never both.

Such architectures have come to be known as LOAD/STORE architectures, and include the machines built by Reduced Instruction Set Computer (RISC) enthusiasts (the IBM 801 [48], Berkeley RISC [47], and Stanford MIPS [35] are prime examples). The design of the instruction pipeline is based on the principle that if an instruction gets past some fixed pipe stage, it should be able to run to completion without incurring any previously unanticipated hazards.

LOAD/STORE architectures are much better at tolerating latencies in memory accesses than are other von Neumann architectures. In order to explain this point, consider a simplified model which detects and avoids hazards in a **LOAD/STORE** architecture similar to the Cray-1. Assume there is a bit associated with every register to indicate that the contents of the register are undergoing a change. The bit corresponding to register R is set the moment an instruction is dispatched which will update R. Following this, instructions are allowed to enter the pipeline only if they don't need to reference or modify register R or other registers reserved in a similar way (a kind of interlocking). Whenever a value is stored in R, the reservation on R is removed. if an instruction is waiting on R, it is allowed to proceed.

This simple scheme works under the assumptions that registers whose values are needed by an instruction are read before the next instruction is dispatched, and that the ALU or the multiple functional units within the ALU are pipelined to accept inputs as fast as the decode stage can supply them, subject to the other kinds of resource and control flow dependences discussed above.

The benefit is that, to the extent memory fetches can be issued far in advance of the need for the data, the latency incurred in the fetches can be masked behind the execution of other, independent instructions. Herein is the hook: the compiler must be able to discover opportunities for fine-grained parallelism in order to separate the memory references from the instructions which use the fetched data. Said another way, the extent to which this technique can be used to mask latency cost depends critically upon the compiler's ability to uncover instruction level parallelism.

An equally necessary requirement for masking latency in this way is proper and efficient hardware support for synchronization (and thus another incestuous linkage between the two fundamental issues). A scheme based on reservation bits on processor registers and associated logic in the instruction dispatcher represents a very basic kind of synchronization support, but such a scheme lacks both scalability and generality. Consider that

- Each fetch requires a target register. Therefore, the degree of parallelism which can be exploited, and thus the latency which can be tolerated, is bounded by the number of registers. Viewed more abstractly, registers are synchronization names, and the small size of the register set artificially constricts the synchronization name space.

- The instruction set lacks the means for expressing this parallelism — the instruction dispatcher must intuit it dynamically, and must be prepared to deal with bad intuition. Specifically, the instruction dispatcher may very quickly find its hands full of instructions which are not quite ready to execute in the search for those which are.

Some LOAD/STORE architectures have eliminated the need for reservation bits on registers by making the compiler responsible for scheduling instructions, such that the result is guaranteed to be available. The compiler can perform hazard resolution only if the time for each operation *e.g.*, ADD, LOAD, is known; it inserts NOP instructions wherever necessary. Because the instruction execution times are an intimate part of the object code, any change to the machine's structure (scaling, redesign) will at the very least require changes to the compiler and regeneration of the code. Current LOAD/STORE architectures assume that memory references either take a fixed amount of time (one cycle in most RISC machines) or that they take a variable but predictable amount of time (as in the Cray-1). In RISC machines, this time is derived on the basis of a cache hit. If the operand is found to be missing from the cache, the pipeline stops. Equivalently, one can think of this as a situation where a clock cycle is stretched to the time required. This solution works because, in most of these machines, there can be either one or a very small number of memory references in progress at any given time. While such schemes reduce the cost of providing synchronization support, they do nothing to solve either the scalability or the generality problems.

Synchronization Methods

Solving latency problems often requires some sort of synchronization mechanism. For this reason, hardware support for synchronization may be justifiable simply because parallel machines are physically partitioned and distributed in space. This Section examines synchronization from a different perspective: having decomposed a program into communicating parts, explicit time-coordination is required which is motivated independently of latency concerns.

To form the basis for a parallel machine, a von Neumann engine must support inter-SQ synchronization in some form, but at what cost and with what granularity? Recall that the cost of any synchronization mechanism will dictate the granularity of the SQ's lest the machine spend all of its time synchronizing. Once the granularity is determined, so is the exploitable parallelism.

Global Scheduling on Synchronous machines. For a given problem on a totally synchronous parallel machine, it is possible to envision a master plan which specifies operations for every cycle on every processor. An analogy can be made between programming such a system and coding a horizontally microprogrammed machine. Recent advances in compiling [27] have made such code generation feasible and have encouraged researchers to propose and build several different synchronous machines [28, 49]. These machines are generally referred to as VERY LONG IN-STRUCTION WORD (VLIW) machines because each instruction actually contains multiple smaller instructions (one per functional unit or processing element). The strategy is based on maximizing the use of resources and resolving potential run-time conflicts in the use of resources at compile time. Memory references and control transfers are "anticipated" as in RISC architectures, but here, multiple concurrent threads of computation are being scheduled instead of only one. Given the possibility of decoding and initiating many instructions in parallel, such architectures are highly appealing when one realizes that the fastest machines available now still essentially decode and dispatch instructions one at a time.

This technique is effective in its currently realized context, *i.e.*, FORTRAN-based computations on a small number (less than several dozen) of processors. Compiling for parallelism beyond this level, however, becomes intractable. It is unclear how problems which rely on dynamic storage allocation or require nondeterministic and real-time constraints will play out on such architectures. It is clear, however, that this technique can and should be combined with other approaches which address dynamic synchronization.

Interrupts and Low-level Context Switching. Almost all von Neumann processors are capable of accepting and handling interrupts. Not surprisingly, parallel machines based on such processors permit the use of inter-processor interrupts as a means for signalling events (*i.e.*, triggering inter-SQ synchronization). However, interrupts are rather expensive because, in general, the processor state needs to be saved. The state-saving may be forced by the hardware as a direct consequence of allowing the interrupt to occur, or it may occur explicitly, *i.e.*, under the control of the programmer, via a single very complex instruction or a suite of less complex ones. Independent of how the state-saving happens, the important thing to note is that each interrupt will generate a significant amount of traffic across the processor / memory interface.

In the previous discussion, it was suggested that larger processor state is helpful in reducing latency cost. Observe, however, that the use of interrupts for inter-SQ synchronization would bid instead for small, easily-switched processor state. Thus, reducing the cost of synchronization by making interrupts cheap would generally entail increasing the cost of memory latency.

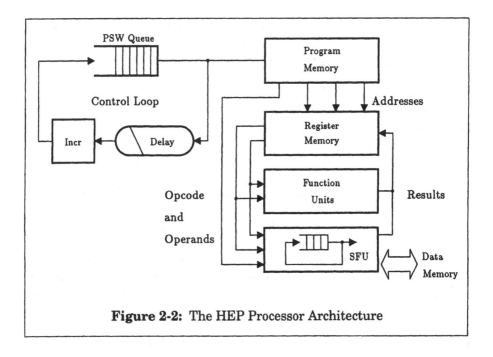

Figure 2-2: The HEP Processor Architecture

Uniprocessors such as the Xerox Alto [59] and the Symbolics 3600 [45] have used the technique of microcode-level context switching to allow sharing of the CPU resource by the I/O device adapters. This is accomplished by duplicating programmer-visible registers, in other words, the processor state. In one microinstruction, the processor can be switched to a new context without causing any state-saving memory references. This dramatically reduces the cost of processing certain types of events that cause frequent interrupts. Few machines have used the idea of keeping multiple hardware-supported instruction contexts in a parallel machine setting, although it should reduce synchronization cost over processors which can hold only a single context. Two important exceptions are the HEP and MASA architectures.

The basic structure of Burton Smith's HEP processor [40, 41] is shown in Figure 2-2. The processor's data path is built as an eight step pipeline. In parallel with the data path is a control loop which circulates process status words (PSW's) of the processes whose threads are to be interleaved for execution. The delay around the control loop varies with the queue size, but is never shorter than eight pipe steps. This minimum value is intentional to allow the PSW at the head of the queue to initiate an instruction but not return again to the head of the queue until the instruction has completed. If at least eight PSW's, representing eight processes, can be kept in the queue, the processor's pipeline will remain full. This scheme is much like traditional pipelining of instructions, but with an important difference. The inter-instruction dependencies are likely to be weaker here because adjacent instructions in the pipe are always from *different processes*.

There are 2048 registers in each processor; each process has an index offset into the register array. Inter-process, *i.e.*, inter-thread, communication is conceptually possible via these registers by overlapping register allocations. The HEP provides *full/empty/reserved* bits on each register and *full/empty* bits on each word in the data memory. An instruction encountering *empty* or *reserved* registers behaves like a NOP instruction; the program counter of the process, *i.e.*, PSW, which initiated the instruction is not incremented. The process effectively busy-waits but without blocking the processor. When a process issues a LOAD or STORE instruction, it is removed from the control loop and is queued separately in the Scheduler Function Unit (SFU) which also issues the memory request. Requests which are not satisfied because of improper *full/empty* status result in recirculation of the PSW within the SFU's loop and also in reissuance of the request. The SFU matches up memory responses with queued PSW's, updates registers as necessary, and reinserts the PSW's in the control loop.

Thus, the HEP is capable up to a point of using parallelism in programs to hide memory and communication latency. At the same time it provides efficient, low-level synchronization mechanisms in the form of presence-bits in registers and main memory. However, the HEP approach does not go far enough because there is a limit of one outstanding memory request per process, and the cost of synchronization involving the registers can be high because of the loss of processor time due to busy-waiting. A serious impediment to software development on the HEP was the limit of 64 PSW's in each processor. Though only 8 PSW's may be required to keep the process pipeline full, a much larger number is needed to name all concurrent tasks of a program.

Experience with the HEP has cast considerable doubt on the usefulness of the registers for inter-thread communication, leading to the conjecture that registers should either be local to a thread, used only between context switches without automatic saving, or eliminated entirely. The HEP experience has reinforced the belief that the low-level synchronization name space should be thought of in terms of the entire address space of a conventional processor and not simply in terms of an unusually large register set. The HEP will be revisited in Section 6.3.

Halstead at MIT and Fujita from NEC Corporation have jointly developed an architecture called MASA which is multithreaded, and intended specifically for parallel symbolic computation [29, 32]. MASA is a tagged architecture in order to support generic operations (with a fully general software trap handling mechanism), parallel, generation-based, incremental garbage collection, and efficient computation with *futures* [31]. From the machine's perspective, a future is a value cell which may either be *unresolved* or *resolved*: initially, a future has no value and hence is unresolved. Subsequent computation can cause the future to mutate (resolve) into a cell which has a value which it retains for the remainder of its lifetime. It is this latter use of tags and associated mechanisms which is particularly novel. MASA provides a number of machine instructions which are nonstrict (*e.g.*, copying, which if given a future as an operand only manipulate the reference to the value cell). These instructions are insensitive to whether the future is resolved or not. For those instructions which are strict in any argument which is a future, execution must either fetch the cell's value if it is resolved, or cause a suspension of the associated task if it is not. The trick, of course, is to perform this so efficiently that the cost of using a future is negligible.

MASA provides explicit hardware resources (called *task frames*) to hold the state of a small number of tasks. This state consists of a small set of general purpose registers along with a program counter, and the identifiers of the parent and one child task frame. Memory words have a synchronizing bit (*full/empty*), but registers are nonsynchronizing. At the beginning of every instruction cycle, the processor may choose among the next instructions of all ready tasks, however, dispatching sequential instructions from a given task incurs a delay equal to the pipeline depth (in the case of the machine currently under study, this is four cycles). Instructions enable a number of trap conditions, which cause dedicated hardware to check tag fields, arithmetic overflow, a synchronization bit, etc., and if an enabled trap condition is met, to NOP the instruction, suspend the task, and invoke a software trap handler.

The HEP-like instruction dispatching scheme of MASA relies on parallelism in excess of the pipe depth at all times in order to avoid dispatching bubbles. Halstead and Fujita recognize the importance of efficient operation in scalar mode, and have outlined strategies which will improve on this dispatching restriction. The practicality of techniques to further reduce this dispatch delay depend on the statistics of trap frequency. With additional study, this will become clearer.

MASA can only name and efficiently switch between a very small number of tasks. The FRAME SAVER does permit tasks to be rolled out and back in; however, the cost of doing so must be considered, and higher level synchronization must be imposed to decide when / what to roll[8]. Again, only execution statistics can demonstrate the significance, or insignificance, of this.

In summary, the limitations of synchronization based on a small number of hardware-supported instruction contexts are clear. High performance processors may have a small programmer-visible state (number of registers) but a much larger implicit state (caches). Low-level context switching does not necessarily take care of the overhead of flushing caches[9]. Further, one can only have a small number of independent contexts without completely overshadowing the cost of the ALU hardware.

Semaphores. A commonly supported feature for synchronization is an atomic operation to test and set the value of a memory location. A processor can signal another processor by writing into a location which the other processor keeps reading to sense a change. Even though, theoretically, it is possible to perform such synchronization with ordinary **READ** and **WRITE** memory operations, the job is much simpler with an atomic **TEST-AND-SET** instruction. **TEST-AND-SET** is powerful enough to implement all types of synchronization paradigms mentioned earlier when combined with higher level software techniques for suspension and resump-

---

[8]This name space limitation is orthogonal to the large producer/consumer synchronization name space (futures as words in a large memory) which is strongly similar to an I-Structure storage name space.

[9]However, solutions such as multicontext caches and multicontext address translation buffers have been used to advantage in reducing this context switching overhead, (c.f., the STO stack mechanism in the IBM 370/168).

tion.   However, the cost of a synchronization scheme based on
TEST-AND-SET can be very high because it normally implies busy waiting.
This results in lost ALU cycles and extra memory references. Implementations of TEST-AND-SET which permit non-busy waiting imply context
switching with the attendant expense.

It is possible to improve upon the behavior of TEST-AND-SET by generaliz-
ing it to the atomic FETCH-AND-OP as suggested by the NYU Ultracomputer group [25]. The instruction requires an address and a value, and
works as follows: suppose two processors, i and j, simultaneously execute
FETCH-AND-ADD instructions with arguments (A,v_i) and (A,v_j) respectively. After one instruction cycle, the contents of A will become $(A)+v_i+v_j$.
Processors i and j will receive, respectively, either (A) and $(A)+v_i$, or $(A)+v_j$
and (A) as results. Indeterminacy is a direct consequence of the race to
update memory cell A.

Different implementations realize different kinds of savings as a result of
using FETCH-AND-OP. The NYU proposal calls for a COMBINING packet
communication network which connects n processors to an n-port memory.
If and when two related packets collide in the network, say
FETCH-AND-ADD(A,v_i) and FETCH-AND-ADD(A,v_j), the switch extracts the
values v_i and v_j, forms a new packet (FETCH-AND-ADD(A,v_i+v_j)), forwards
it to the memory, and stores the value of v_i temporarily. When the
memory returns the old value of location A, the switch returns two values
$((A)$ and $(A)+v_i)$.

This has the effect of reducing the total number of network packets in
transit and of limiting the number of fetch requests converging on a given
memory address. Some synchronization situations which would have
taken $O(n)$ time can be done in $O(\log n)$ time. It should be noted, however,
that one memory reference may involve as many as $\log_2 n$ additions, and
implies substantial hardware complexity. Moreover, neither the abstract
notion of FETCH-based synchronization nor its combining implementation
addresses the general case of efficient suspension and resumption. It is
possible that providing such a facility without additional hardware support will be inefficient to the point of completely overshadowing the
benefit of space-distributed atomic operations.

In the Cedar project [43], combining happens in the memory controller.

This results in a similar limitation of fetches against an address, but does nothing to reduce network packets. Implementation in software by interpretation is a logically possible third alternative, but realizes little, if any benefit.

In none of these schemes is the issue of using parallelism and efficient synchronization to hide latency addressed. In the worst case, the complexity of hardware support for combining may actually increase the latency.

Cache Coherence Mechanisms. While highly successful for reducing memory latency in uniprocessors, caches in a parallel machine setting introduce a serious synchronization problem called CACHE COHERENCE. Censier and Feautrier [17] define the problem as follows:

> A memory scheme is coherent if the value returned on a LOAD instruction is always the value given by the latest STORE instruction with the same address.

It is easy to see that this may be difficult to achieve in a parallel machine.

Consider a two-processor system tightly coupled through a single main memory. Each processor has its own cache to which it has exclusive access. Suppose further that two program fragments are running, one on each processor, and it is known that the fragments are designed to communicate through one or more shared memory cells. In the absence of caches, this scheme can be made to work. If, on the other hand, it happens that the shared address is present in both caches, the individual processors can read from and write to the address and never see any changes caused by the other processor. Using a store-through design instead of a store-in design does not solve the problem either. What is logically required is a mechanism which, upon the occurrence of a STORE to location x, invalidates copies of location x in caches of other processors, and guarantees that subsequent LOADs will get the most recent (cached) value. This can incur significant overhead in terms of decreased memory bandwidth.

Solutions to the cache coherence problem center around reducing the cost of detecting the possibility of incoherence, typically by using a logical directory of cached data. Each entry in the directory reflects the state of the associated cache line, *e.g.*, private, read-only, shared, etc. The directory is updated as necessary when lines change state, and can be used to detect the possibility of incoherence. For example, when an attempt is made to write to a shared line, the directory detects the need to inform others to purge their copies. Obviously, a centralized implementation of the directory does not scale. The directory may be distributed, and in some cases the state information can be stored economically as a few extra bits on each cache line. The problem now becomes one of keeping the distributed directory itself coherent. Many opportunities exist to reduce the amount of coherence-maintaining communication based on the state information (*e.g.*, writing to a cache line marked as private requires no communication), but some nontrivial communication will always be required[10], and the amount of communication will likely not diminish as a machine is scaled. The machine's performance will ultimately be limited by the rate at which directories can process this coherence-maintaining traffic from their peers. Many other schemes have been proposed for handling caches in small-degree parallel machines such as making caches partially visible to the programmer, allowing explicit state annotation and explicit flushing of lines.

It is worth noting that, while not obvious, a direct trade-off often exists between decreasing the parallelism and increasing the cachable or non-shared data. It is further noteworthy that latency and synchronization are inextricably intertwined here: to reduce latency, caches are introduced. This results in a synchronization problem (coherence). Solutions to the synchronization problem such as implicit and explicit purging of cache lines will result in poorer cache hit rates and increased average latency.

Analysis and Summary

The von Neumann model, by virtue of its simplicity, offers some tremendous advantages. Consider, for example, that given the static structure of a compiled program and nothing more than the value of the program counter during execution, a tremendous amount of information can be deduced, *e.g.*, the satisfaction or lack thereof of data dependences, the termination of predecessor instructions, the non-initiation of successor in-

---

[10]One exception is the case of embarrassingly parallel applications which decompose into non-communicating SQ's.

structions, and so on. Consider also that a sequential thread of computation, occupying a pipeline, has, by definition, exclusive access to the entire state of the underlying machinery. This implies that the cost of communicating data values between instructions can be made extraordinarily low, and that the compiler has tremendous leverage in managing the machine state per its own criteria of optimality. Do these facts in any way imply that von Neumann machines should be the basis for scalable, general purpose parallel computing?

Advocates of non-von Neumann architectures (including the author) have argued that the notion of sequential instruction execution is the antithesis of parallel processing. This criticism is actually slightly off the mark. Rather, a von Neumann processor in a parallel machine configuration does poorly because it fails to provide efficient synchronization support at a level low enough to permit its liberal and free use. Why is this so?

Traditionally, the synchronization meeting ground has taken the form of a semaphore [18], a register [50], a buffer tag [55], an interrupt level, or any of a number of similar devices. When viewed as a name space, it should be clear that the number of simultaneously pending synchronization events is bounded by a rather small integer, and therefore the amount of exploitable parallelism faces a severe hardware-imposed limit.

When the cost of each synchronization action is also counted, it should be equally clear that any attempt to exploit fine-grained parallelism will be quite expensive if not impossible in a realistic sense. These synchronization mechanisms are inherently larger grain (*e.g.*, interrupts) or involve busy waiting (*e.g.*, the HEP [40, 52]). Therefore, the cost of each event is quite high. Such mechanisms are unsuitable for controlling latency cost. Moreover, since suspension and resumption typically involve expensive context switching, exploitation of parallelism by decomposing a program into many small, communicating tasks may not actually realize a speedup. In terms of Figure 1-6, the FORK/JOIN costs C_f and C_j may be unbounded as in the case of busy waiting. In the best of cases they may be bounded, but mean values of 10^3 to 10^5 instructions are typical, thereby limiting the minimum useful SQ size to something on this order.

It is important to observe that these arguments together favor the alteration of the basic von Neumann mechanism, and not its total abandonment.

For situations where instruction sequencing and data dependence constraints can be worked out at compile time, there is still reason to believe
that a von Neumann style sequential (deterministic time order) interpreter provides better control over the machine's behavior than does a
dynamic scheduling mechanism and, arguably, better performance/cost. It
is only in those situations where sequencing cannot be so optimized at
compile time, e.g., for long latency operations, that dynamic scheduling
and low-level synchronization are called for. One must also keep in mind
that, despite any desire to revolutionize computer architecture, von
Neumann machines will continue to be the best understood base upon
which to build for many years.

2.2 DATAFLOW ARCHITECTURES

Dataflow architectures [3, 23, 30, 36] represent a radical alternative to
von Neumann architectures because they use dataflow graphs as their
machine language [5, 22]. Dataflow graphs, as opposed to conventional
machine languages, specify only a partial order on the execution of instructions and thus provide opportunities for parallel and pipelined execution at the level of individual instructions. For example, the dataflow
graph for the expression

   (a*b) + (c*d)

only specifies that both multiplications be executed before the addition.
The multiplications can be executed in any order, even in parallel. The
advantage of this flexibility becomes apparent when considering that the
order in which a,b,c and d become available may not be known at compile
time. For example, computations for operands a and b may take longer
than computations for c and d.

The instruction execution mechanism of a dataflow processor is fundamen-
tally different from that of a von Neumann processor. Consider the MIT
Tagged-Token architecture, as depicted in Figure 2-3. Rather than using
a program counter to determine the next instruction to be executed and
then fetching operands accordingly, a dataflow machine provides a low-
level synchronization mechanism in the form of a WAITING-MATCHING
store which dispatches only those instructions for which data are already
available. This mechanism relies on TAGGING each datum with the address of the instruction to which it belongs and the context in which the

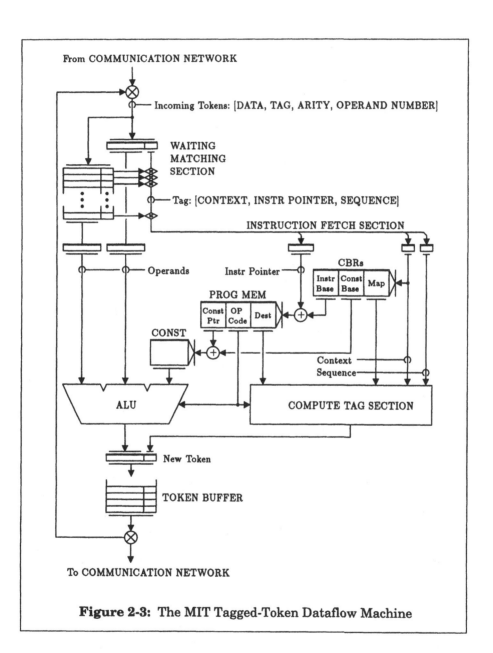

Figure 2-3: The MIT Tagged-Token Dataflow Machine

instruction is to be executed. One can think of the instruction address as replacing the program counter, and the context identifier as replacing the traditional frame base register. It is the machine's job to match up data with identical tags and then to execute the denoted instruction. In so doing, a new datum will be produced, with a new tag indicating the successor instruction(s). Thus, each instruction represents a synchronization operation. Note that the number of synchronization names is limited by the size of the tag, which is intentionally large. Note also that the processor pipeline is non-blocking: given that the operands for an instruction are available, the corresponding instruction can be executed without further synchronization.

In addition to the Waiting-Matching Section which is used primarily for dynamic scheduling of instructions, the MIT Tagged-Token machine provides a second synchronization mechanism called I-STRUCTURE STORAGE [33]. Each word of I-structure storage has two state bits associated with it to indicate whether the word is *empty*, *written* or *deferred*, *i.e.*, that it has pending read requests against it. This greatly facilitates overlapped execution of a producer of a data structure with the consumer of that data structure. There are three instructions at the graph level to manipulate I-structure storage. These are **ALLOCATE** to allocate an array of n empty words of storage, **I-FETCH** to fetch the contents of the ith word of an array, and **I-STORE** to store a value in a specified word. Generally, software concerns dictate that a word be written into only once before it is deallocated.

The dataflow processor treats all I-structure operations as split transactions (discussed more fully in Section 3.1). For example, when the **I-FETCH** instruction is executed, a packet containing the tag of the destination instruction of the **I-FETCH** is forwarded to the proper I-structure storage address, possibly in a distant I-structure storage module. The actual memory operation may require waiting if the datum is not present, and thus the result may be returned many instruction times later. The key is that the instruction pipeline need not be suspended during this time. Rather, processing of other instructions may continue immediately after initiation of the operation. Matching of memory responses with waiting instructions is done via tags in the Waiting-Matching Section.

One advantage of tagging each datum is that data from different contexts can be mixed freely in the instruction execution pipeline. Thus, instruction-level parallelism of dataflow graphs can effectively absorb the communication latency and minimize the losses due to synchronization waits.

In summary, the MIT Tagged Token Dataflow Architecture (TTDA), and other dataflow architectures like it [30, 36], provide well-integrated synchronization at a very basic level. In terms of Figure 1-6, the costs C_f and C_j are both less than one, depending upon how the counting is done[11]. By using an encoded dataflow graph for program representation, machine instructions become self-sequencing. Said another way, interpreting a DFPG on a dataflow machine means treating each primitive graph instruction as its own SQ. All of the synchronization and instruction dispatching is dynamic. One strength of the TTDA is that each datum carries its own context identifying information. By this mechanism, program parallelism can be easily traded for latency because there is no additional cost above and beyond this basic mechanism for switching contexts on a per-instruction basis.

However, it is clear that not all of the distinguishing characteristics of the TTDA contribute towards efficient toleration of latency and synchronization costs. One very sound criticism is that intra-procedure communication is unnecessarily general. Intuitively, it should not be necessary to create and match tokens for scheduling every instruction within the body of a procedure — some scheduling can certainly be done by the compiler, for example, in the evaluation of an arithmetic expression. In a dataflow machine, however, data driven scheduling is *de rigueur*.

The notion of a nonblocking, context-interleaving pipeline is a two-edged sword. It provides the ultimate flexibility in context switching, but implies that the notion of locality must be reconsidered. Again by intuition, given a full dataflow pipeline of depth n, the sizes of instruction and operand buffers or caches which guarantee a given hit rate (called the WORKING SET SIZE) must be on the order of the sum of the n working set sizes for the threads of computation which coexist in the pipe. Also, from

---

[11]Each abstract machine instruction is capable of doing a JOIN, some computation, and a FORK.

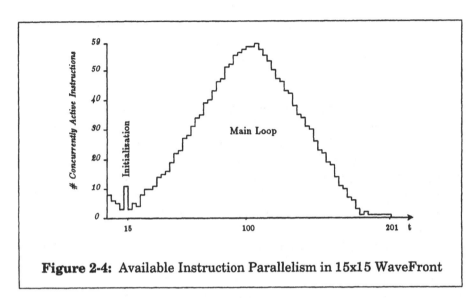

Figure 2-4: Available Instruction Parallelism in 15x15 WaveFront

the previous Chapter, machines which support only explicit instruction scheduling, such as pure dataflow machines, perform poorly on sequential code sections. The time to execute the instructions in a graph's critical path is n times the critical path length. One is left to wonder if it might not be possible, even desirable, to optimize this by performing the necessary synchronization explicitly, and relying on more traditional (read: *well-understood*) mechanisms for instruction sequencing in the remainder of the cases. The uncertainties in this argument are the fraction of time wherein synchronization is necessary, and the complexity of the mechanisms required.

2.3 COMPARISON OF APPROACHES

It is illustrative to consider an example program and to examine the kinds of parallelism which can be exploited under the von Neumann and dataflow models. The available parallelism in an ideal situation as a function of time can be plotted as a PARALLELISM PROFILE[12]. Figure 2-4 is the parallelism profile for the WaveFront program for a 15×15 array.

---

[12]Parallelism profiles are derived by compiling a program into a dataflow graph of primitive instructions, *e.g.*, ADD, which preserves only the essential data dependences. The compiled graph is interpreted, with each instruction in the graph taking unit time. Intercommunication latencies are assumed to be zero. At any time step, all and only those instructions which are logically enabled are executed. The profile plots the number of such instructions as a function of time.

The small blips around $t=15$ represent initialization of the first row and first column of the array. The bulk of the execution time belongs to the doubly-nested loop which performs the wavefront computation proper. As expected, the parallelism rises essentially linearly until the computation diagonal reaches the middle of the array (corresponding to the linear increase in number of elements computed on the wave front). After this point, a corresponding linear decline is seen.

The parallelism exposed here takes a number of forms. While it is beyond the scope and intent of this work to discuss the linguistic underpinnings which make the exposure of parallelism possible, it is useful and instructive to examine the types of parallelism which combine to give the results here:

- At the most basic level, the expression in the loop body has a certain amount of parallelism built into it. Given the loop variables i and j, three elements can be fetched from the two-dimensional array m in parallel (recall the DFPG for WaveFront's inner loop body in Figure 1-2). Such parallelism is difficult to exploit across processors, but as is discussed later, this class of parallelism is essential for keeping the pipeline full in the presence of long latencies.

- At a higher level, multiple instances of the inner loop are active simultaneously.

- Higher yet, multiple iterations of the outer loop are concurrently active. It is the outer iteration which spawns multiple inner loop instances.

A dataflow machine which supports I-Structure storage can easily exploit all three forms of parallelism. The dynamic result is that each diagonal is the producer of data consumed by the next diagonal. Moreover, a dataflow machine can exploit additional producer / consumer overlap between multiple, dependent instances of the same program. Consider the MultiWave program below:

```
def multiwave edge_vector n =
  {m = wavefront edge_vector;
   in
     {for i from 1 to n do
        next m = wave m;
      finally m}};
```

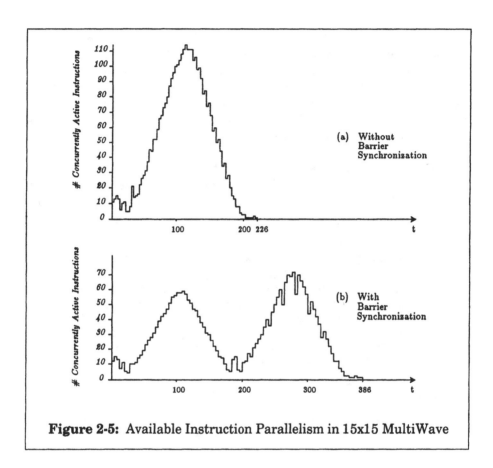

Figure 2-5: Available Instruction Parallelism in 15x15 MultiWave

Here, the function Wave is similar to WaveFront above, except that the input is the matrix produced by WaveFront instead of an initialization vector, and that the loop body is changed thus:

```
m[i,j] = (m[i-1,j] +
          m[i,j-1] +
          m[i-1,j-1] +
          previous_matrix[i,j]) / 4;}}
```

That is, a dependence on history has been added: the computation of $m[i,j]$ now makes reference to its previous value. The parallelism profile is shown in Figure 2-5a. When it is realized that a dataflow machine can exploit this parallelism as well, the result is quite remarkable. The peak (and average) parallelisms have simply doubled, and the critical path time has increased a mere 12.4% (*c.f.*, Figure 2-4).

Needless to say, a traditional von Neumann machine would be able to exploit virtually none of this parallelism without significant effort. First of all, the program would have to be expressed differently. In the Id approach, it is quite correct to think the program is giving a definition for the value of each cell, and that the time-ordering of instructions necessary to compute that value is dynamically determined by the dataflow hardware. It is therefore transparent to the programmer.

The point that von Neumann architecture offers a very different paradigm is clearly made if one considers transliterating the Id code to FORTRAN. There, the program becomes a specification of how to compute instead of what to compute. Simply iterating over rows and columns, FORTRAN semantics would in fact hide the opportunity for inner loop parallelism because there is a data dependence between inner loop iterations (consider the first invocation of the inner loop with $i=l$ and $j=l..u$). Loop interchange won't help in this situation. The program would have to be re-coded to literally express computing the diagonals, with each inner loop instance running along one diagonal. Aside from the aesthetics of doing this, it is hard to argue that such transformations could be done automatically with any degree of generality.

Given that the program can be re-coded by some means [4], the question of what kinds of parallelism are exploitable remains. It is conceivable that a compiler could exploit some amount of expression-level parallelism through instruction reordering with the objective of partially masking latency cost. It is also conceivable that inter-iteration parallelism in the inner loop (one iteration corresponding to the computation of one element in a diagonal) could be exploited, say, by the use of vector instructions.

It is difficult to imagine an efficient way, however, of exploiting the outer loop parallelism depicted in Figure 2-5a without further re-coding because of the required fine-grained synchronization. At best, the compiler would have to enforce barrier synchronization at the end of each outer loop iteration before letting the next iteration begin. The effect of such a barrier can be simulated by introducing an inter-iteration dependence on the availability of the lower-right element in the matrix. The not-too-surprising result for two iterations is shown in Figure 2-5b. Given n iterations over an $m \times m$ array, the best-case running time is proportional to $m \times n$. Under the dataflow model (Figure 2-5a), however, the best-case running

time is proportional to *m+n*.   The cost of not having fine-grained
synchronization support is clear, yet from the criticism of dataflow architectures, the cost of one such type of fine-grained synchronization is
also clear.

2.4 SUMMARY

Processor architecture plays a critically important role in the making of a
parallel machine. Dataflow architectures embody something which is sufficient for tolerating low-level latencies while simultaneously providing
fine-grained synchronization support to programs decomposed for parallelism. While von Neumann machines are clearly superior in the execution of long sequential threads, the inability to provide cheap, fine-grained
synchronization has left doubts as to whether von Neumann architecture
can reasonably be a basis for building parallel machines. A very basic
shortcoming arises because memory latency determines the time to execute memory reference instructions. Said another way, von Neumann instruction sets are traditionally designed with instructions whose execution
time is latency dependent. When this latency cannot be hidden by some
means, a tangible performance penalty is incurred. Moreover, von
Neumann instruction execution is implicitly synchronized by the
dispatching circuitry, using a program counter for sequential instruction
initiation. In a parallel computer, a qualitatively different kind of
synchronization is required between tasks due to their assumed mutual
asynchrony.

The obvious question is *can a new architecture be synthesized out of the
best features of dataflow and von Neumann architectures which adequately
addresses the shortfalls of both?* Arvind has suggested that an architecture formed on the principles of split transaction I-Structure memory
references in a von Neumann framework, coupled with data driven res-
cheduling of suspended instructions would be a reasonable starting point
for investigating this question. Such a machine has the potential of
tolerating memory latency and of supporting fine-grained synchronization
and yet, in the strict sense, is neither a von Neumann machine nor a
dataflow machine. In the next Chapter, this question is explored.

Chapter Three

A Dataflow / von Neumann Hybrid

3.1 SYNTHESIS

In the previous Chapter, it was concluded that satisfactory solutions to the problems raised for von Neumann architectures can only be had by altering the architecture of the processor itself. It was further observed that dataflow architectures do address these problems satisfactorily. Based on observations of the near-miss behavior of certain von Neumann parallel processors (*e.g.*, the Denelcor HEP [40, 52]), it is reasonable to speculate that dataflow and von Neumann machines actually represent two points on a continuum of architectures. The goal of the present study is to develop a new machine model which differs minimally from the von Neumann model, yet embodies the same latency and synchronization characteristics which make dataflow architectures amenable to parallel processing.

Starting with the observation that the costs associated with dataflow instruction sequencing in many instances are excessive, others have suggested that dataflow ideas should be used only at the inter-procedural level [42] thereby avoiding dataflow inefficiencies while seemingly retaining certain advantages. This view is almost correct, but ignores the importance of the fundamental issues. Restricting architectures to this "macro dataflow" concept would amount to giving up what is possibly a dataflow machine's biggest feature — the ability to context switch efficiently at a low level to cover memory latency.

Given this, one is led to ask the following question: *what mechanisms at the hardware level are essential for tolerating latency and synchronization costs?* Based on various studies of parallel machines [2, 14, 21, 40] and on the observations presented thus far, the following conclusions are drawn:

- In general, on a machine capable of supporting multiple simultaneous SQ instances, executing programs expressed as a total ordering of instructions will incur more latency cost than will executing a logically equivalent partial ordering of the same instructions. In fact, for any lenient programming language [58], expressing programs as a partial ordering is a necessary condition for avoiding deadlock. It is assumed, therefore, that the machine language of any scalable, general purpose parallel computer must be able to express partial ordering.

- In any parallel machine architecture, certain operations will take an unbounded amount of time to complete (*e.g.*, those involving communication). Such operations can be either atomic, single phase operations or split transaction, multiphase operations. A SPLIT TRANSACTION is an operation which can be divided into parts which separately initiate the operation and later synchronize prior to using the result. Split transaction processing will always minimize latency cost over single phase processing because the potential exists for covering processor idle time. Based on the frequency of the occurrence of such long latency operations [2] in all but the most trivial parallel computations, efficient split transaction operation requires specific hardware mechanisms [7, 21].

The architecture developed in this Chapter embodies these beliefs and reconciles the criticisms of von Neumann and dataflow architectures. This architecture is characterized by its machine language which can be viewed as a superset of both von Neumann and dataflow machine languages. The term PARALLEL MACHINE LANGUAGE (PML) will be used to describe this superset. A proper PML must have the following characteristics:

- The execution time for any given instruction must be independent of latency. Traditional latency-sensitive operations, *e.g.*, LOADs from memory, must be re-phrased as split transactions.

- Synchronization meeting places and synchronization participants must be named. Names must be drawn from a large name space.

- Means for expressing both implicit (*i.e.*, program counter based) and explicit (named, dynamic) synchronization must be provided.

The remainder of this Chapter is devoted to the definition of a PML (Section 3.2) and to the definition of a concrete architecture which executes it efficiently (Section 3.3).

3.2 COMPILATION TARGET MODEL

In this Section, the notion of a parallel machine language is developed as a basis for general-purpose parallel computing. Such a language provides a metaphor for parallel SQ execution which must encompass means for naming SQ instances and means for time-coordinating, or synchronizing the instances. A key idea is that the SQ size should not be bound by the parallel machine language but rather that the machine language should support SQ's of arbitrary size in a completely general way.

While the focus of this work is not on languages and compilers for general purpose parallel computers, it is convenient to make use of extant languages and tools for the purpose of assisting in the development and characterization of the architecture. To that end, Id and its compiler have been used in this study. This choice has brought with it certain complications (discussed later), but provides a flexible vehicle for generating dataflow graphs from a high level language. DFPG's are assumed as the preferred starting point in generating PML code. The approach will be to consider how dataflow graphs can be re-represented so as to express both implicit and explicit synchronization.

A Suitable Program Representation

From the previous Chapters, it has become clear that DFPG's are a powerful abstract representation for parallel programs. However, direct interpretation of DFPG-derived graphs as in a dataflow machine implies that all synchronization should be dynamic. It has been shown that this leads to poor performance on sequential code sections. It is imperative that the representation of the program at the level of the machine should permit specification of both traditional sequential instruction dispatch and dynamic scheduling based on run-time synchronization support. Graph-based representations are sufficient for this task given the view that a graph can be partitioned, and that partitions can be executed sequentially. Conforming to the previous notation, partitions will be called scheduling quanta (SQ's) because their sequential semantics are consistent with the notion of a *unit of schedulability*.

Providing an architectural notion of partitioning, *i.e.*, supporting SQ's of arbitrary length, is a step beyond both dataflow and von Neumann architectures. In the dataflow paradigm, each instruction is its own SQ. In the von Neumann case, at least with conventional languages, the entire compiled program is the SQ[13].

It is reasonable to hypothesize that the partitioning methodology should not be bound by the architecture as it is in both the dataflow and von Neumann cases. Rather, partitioning should be left as a degree of freedom for the compiler, and the architecture should provide explicit support for this. That is, an architecture should not be judged on its stated partitioning stance but rather on its support for a variety of methods (sequential, fine-grained parallel, coarse-grained parallel, etc.). Such an architecture must, therefore, simultaneously support efficient sequential threads of execution and multiple execution contexts with minimal costs for naming and synchronizing.

Support for Synchronization

Synchronization in the von Neumann architecture is both a very old and a relatively new notion. In the strictest sense, synchronization has always been necessary for correct operation — operands must always be produced before they are consumed. However, under sequential execution semantics, synchronization is implicit in instruction ordering. Having concluded that programs should be expressed as a partial order of SQ's invalidates this assumption, and explicit means must be provided. In general it is not possible to impose a total ordering on a set of SQ's[14]. Inter-SQ sequencing can only be determined at run time.

Architectural support for synchronization and scheduling of SQ's depends on a number of issues, but the most basic is that of strictness. Within any arbitrary grouping of instructions, it is possible, even likely, that the total input requirement for the SQ will exceed that of the first instruction. The architecture may provide strict scheduling where all SQ inputs must be present prior to invoking the SQ, or nonstrict scheduling where invocation is based solely on the requirements of the instruction to be executed next.

---

[13]Compiling dataflow graphs derived from functional languages for a von Neumann machine will force the issue in that SQ's will in many cases have to be much smaller than the entire program. This will imply some sort of interpretive mechanism to schedule the SQ's with the attendant overhead. See Traub [58] for a fuller treatment.

[14]This in essence is von Neumann instruction sequencing and, with lenient programming languages such as Id, may lead to deadlock.

The former case is explored by Buehrer and Ekanadham [15]. It seems likely that, given a set of synchronization requirements and the need to express these succinctly, support for strict scheduling will result in a larger number of smaller SQ's than will nonstrict scheduling. This conjecture follows from the observation that it is not possible to transform a nonstrict partition into a strict one simply by moving all synchronizations to the beginning of an SQ without introducing the possibility of deadlock. It will be necessary to split the larger, nonstrict SQ's into separate smaller ones at the intermediate synchronization points. Moreover, given a nonstrict scheduling mechanism, the compiler can choose to partition so as to mimic the behavior of strict scheduling. For the sake of this study, then, the more general nonstrict scheduling policy is assumed. It is further assumed that synchronization overhead, whatever the mechanism, is efficient to the extreme of not being a first-order concern in code generation. Moreover, it is assumed that a large, global synchronization name space is available, and that the cost of allocating names from this space is also negligible[15].

The instruction firing rules under this scheduling discipline must guarantee that instructions do not execute until the required inputs are present. In a dataflow machine, this simply means that appropriate tokens (operands) must arrive on all input arcs in order for an instruction to fire, and the detection of arrival is a run-time action taken by the hardware. In a machine which supports arbitrary SQ's, the constraint of operand arrival must still be satisfied. However, the dataflow mechanism is not the ideal choice in that it is impossible to distinguish operands on the basis of their origin. In reality, only some of them require synchronization at run time. Having partitioned a graph into a set of nontrivial SQ's[16], it is possible to distinguish different type of arcs

> **Definition 3-1:** A STATIC UNSYNCHRONIZED ARC is any explicit arc between two instructions in the same SQ.

For such arcs, the synchronization constraint can be satisfied via proper instruction ordering within the SQ. That is, sequential execution within

---

[15]In later Chapters, these assumptions will be tested.

[16]A trivial SQ contains no instructions or has no input/output dependence relationships with other SQ'S.

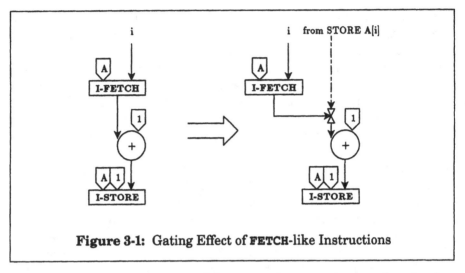

Figure 3-1: Gating Effect of **FETCH**-like Instructions

the SQ captures the constraint of the arc, and no run time synchronization is necessary.

Definition 3-2: A STATIC SYNCHRONIZED ARC is any explicit arc between two instructions in different SQ's.

For such arcs, the sequencing constraint can only be satisfied, in general, by some dynamic mechanism in that SQ executions are not totally ordered. There are interesting special cases of arcs crossing SQ boundaries which do not require run time synchronization; these will be discussed in Section 5.1.

While not expressed explicitly in a dataflow program graph, there is an implicit dynamic arc between every **I-STORE** instruction and **I-FETCH** instruction which refer to the same structure and element (recall I-Structure semantics from Section 2.2). The arc is properly drawn from the output of the **I-STORE** to the input of the **I-FETCH** only in the sense that the output of the **I-FETCH** appears, at the graph level, to be strict in this "input." However, the desired behavior of **I-FETCH**, as discussed below, is that the **I-FETCH** operation itself should not depend upon the state of the slot (*e.g.*, **Empty**) from which a value is being fetched. **I-FETCH** should merely initiate the fetching, and some kind of synchronization mechanism must guarantee that instructions to receive the result of the fetch do not execute until the value is indeed available. Hence, the arc from the **I-STORE** is gated by the execution of the **I-FETCH**, as depicted in Figure 3-1.

Every instruction which exhibits this kind of implicit, synchronizing behavior will be treated specially.

> **Definition 3-3:** A FETCH-LIKE OUTPUT of an instruction is one
> which gates a dynamic arc connecting an I-STORE-like instruc-
> tion with the sink instruction which is to receive its value. An
> instruction itself is FETCH-like if at least one of its outputs is
> FETCH-like.

As shall become clear below, a FETCH-like output is an abstraction of a
synchronized, long-latency operation. The actual dynamic arc begins at
the I-STORE, and terminates at the virtual gate. A static arc connects the
virtual gate to each sink instruction. There is, clearly, a one-to-one correspondence between these arcs and the actual arcs in the graph which
connect I-FETCH instructions to the sinks. These arcs have particular significance.

> **Definition 3-4:** A DYNAMIC SYNCHRONIZED ARC is any arc
> which connects a FETCH-like output to a sink instruction.

The problem of managing synchronized arcs is analogous to the problem of
coordinating producers and consumers at a higher level by the use of I-
structure storage [33]. The idea is to associate state bits with each slot in
such a storage which indicate written or unwritten status. When written,
read operations perform as in a normal memory. When unwritten, read
operations are deferred; operationally, the read request itself is stored in
the offending slot to wait for a write request to come along. When this
happens, the deferred read request is satisfied by forwarding the newly arrived value. Significant time may elapse between arrival of the read request and arrival of the write request. This is of no consequence to the I-
structure storage unit *per se*. In the event that multiple read requests
must be deferred, a list is created and associated with the slot. This
causes practical, but not conceptual, problems. Engineering solutions
depend on the statistics of list length which are related to a number of factors.

This idea can be applied to the problem of synchronizing SQ invocations.
With each invocation of a procedure is associated an array of slots called a
FRAME. A slot is provided for the output of each instruction in the

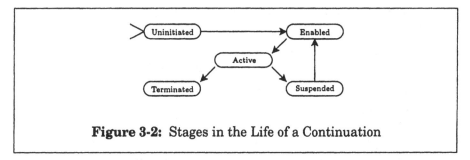

Figure 3-2: Stages in the Life of a Continuation

procedure[17]. Each slot has I-structure-store-like behavior in that the slot has state bits (called presence bits) indicating its emptiness or fullness, and sequential processing of a continuation makes use of these presence bits to effect synchronization action.

Continuations can be thought of as being in one of the states depicted in Figure 3-2. Upon initiation, a continuation becomes enabled. Enabled continuations compete for processor resources, and eventually become active when scheduled. The active continuation on each processor executes instructions sequentially and is free to use any and all of the resources on that processor. Synchronization action is effected by testing the presence bits of one or more slots in the frame, *i.e.*, by the fetching of operands. Fetching from an empty slot causes the active continuation to enter the suspended state, whereupon another enabled continuation may become active. The fact of the suspension is recorded in the empty slot itself. A subsequent **STORE** operation into the slot causes the previously suspended continuation to re-enter the enabled state[18]. A continuation may be suspended a number of times between initiation and termination. One can think of a continuation as behaving like a more traditional task in a demand paged system which, upon encountering a missing memory page, becomes suspended until the page is made available.

---

[17]While not considered here, re-use of slots within an invocation's frame is possible. The problem is similar to that of re-using registers with the exception that reference patterns are often not statically determined. That is, the problem of deciding when the last reference to a slot has been made to permit re-use is dependent upon the time-ordering of the execution of asynchronous SQ instances.

[18]Like I-structure storage, values may be fetched repeatedly. Fetching does not, in general, reset the presence bits.

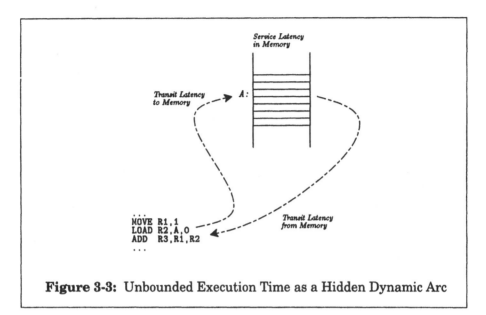

Figure 3-3: Unbounded Execution Time as a Hidden Dynamic Arc

Latency

With this powerful hardware-level synchronization technique, it is straightforward to devise a method of tolerating long latencies. Dynamic synchronized arcs represent the instances of latencies which cannot be bounded at compile time, and always occur at the outputs of instructions which initiate long latency operations. Within the von Neumann paradigm, it is most commonly the case that such long latencies are embedded in instructions and directly result in processor idle time (Figure 3-3). In order to prevent long latencies from causing the processor to idle, the following is assumed:

> **Proposition 3-5:** Dynamic synchronized arcs must never occur within a non-preemptible unit of execution, and may only exist between such units of execution.

In a von Neumann machine, this condition is violated because instructions are in general non-preemptible and may contain dynamic synchronized arcs, *e.g.*, LOAD. There are certainly some exceptions to non-preemption. The IBM System/370 architecture [38] recognizes that system integrity is a function of bounded I/O interrupt response time and, therefore, instructions which may run for a long time, *e.g.*, Move Long (MVCL), are can be preempted (actually segmented) at well-defined intermediate points. Note that the time between such segment boundaries is much longer (*e.g.*, 256 memory cycles) than average instruction execution time. Such preemption might be useful in solving the latency problem if only it were available for all instructions which embed long latency arcs (again, **LOAD**), but this is not the case for von Neumann machines in general.

The proposition can be narrowed to say that *dynamic synchronized arcs must never be embedded in the semantics of an instruction*. That is, instruction execution time must never be a function of unpredictable latency. This is most easily guaranteed by splitting all instructions with embedded dynamic arcs into two parts which separately initiate and then synchronize. In the case of **LOAD**ing a value from a remote memory unit, one instruction would simply initiate the **FETCH** without waiting for the value to arrive. It would then be the responsibility of any instructions which use the **FETCH**ed value to synchronize, or check for its presence, before proceeding. This is the fundamental difference between the operation which retrieves a value from I-Structure Storage, **I-FETCH**, and the traditional pipeline-blocking memory reference instructions from von Neumann architecture. Long-latency instructions must be phrased as split transactions to facilitate the masking of latency cost.

In the context of the present discussion, it is useful to view these arcs as hinge-points between units of execution (SQ's). Specifically, the Proposition mandates the movement of the instances of unbounded latencies so that they occur only between rather than within SQ's. The intuition is that while SQ *A* may initiate a number of long-latency operations, in order to mask the effect of the latency, the consumers of the long-latency results must be asynchronous to *A*. This notion will be refined in Chapter 4. In this way, the proposition may be phrased that *dynamic synchronized arcs must never occur inside an SQ*. The partitioning of a graph must in some way be based on the dynamic synchronized arcs within it.

It is therefore assumed that all long latency instructions will be split transactions. In this model, the initiating instruction causes enough information to be sent, say, to the memory subsystem so that the result can be sent back and stored into an appropriate frame slot. Any attempt to use the value prior to its arrival in this slot will result in suspension as described above. Note that the remote storage unit itself need not be an I-structure storage for this mechanism to work properly, but one is assumed nevertheless. By this assumption, the first requirement for PML's is satisfied.

Overview of the Model

In this section, the proposal for a hybrid machine is made more concrete by presenting a specific pipeline organization and compilation model. This is convenient for expository reasons, and it is essential to enable the verification and analysis in subsequent Chapters.

The compilation model is intended to be representative of a variety of RISC-style von Neumann machines, to which one might add mechanisms for dealing with SQ's. The model is based on a three-address instruction set, with operands fetched from frame slots, stored in a memory which is purely local to a given processor. A small set of registers is also available for operand storage. The registers are not part of the private state of an SQ instance (continuation) but rather are shared across them. This assumption is significant in that the architecture provides no automatic save/restore facility and, therefore, registers cannot be used to hold computation state across potential suspensions. The goal is to avoid the need to save and restore registers by exploiting the hybrid nature of the PML representation — sequences of register-dependent von Neumann style code combined with the asynchronous, register-independent dataflow code[19].

Hardware Types. While specifics of hardware data types and number systems are somewhat orthogonal to the architectural issues of interest in this study, it is difficult to make convincing arguments about performance and efficiency without taking some stand on many of these. For this reason, the following assumptions are made. While it was expedient in the implementation of arithmetic to assume that types are explicitly represented at the hardware level, this issue is unimportant for the points

---

[19]Intuition may lead one to believe that such a scheme results in degraded performance over a pure von Neumann machine in the form of additional memory references for loading and unloading registers. As shall become clear in a later Section, this is an oversimplification because frame storage can be cached easily without a coherence problem.

to be made and can be ignored[20].   That is, while each instruction's
operand types are explicitly defined, the architecture under study takes no
stand on the issue of hardware typing.

The following hardware types are defined.   Each is a word-sized object
which can fit into a register or local memory slot:

INTEGER (*INT*):   Two's complement encoding.

FLOATING POINT NUMBER (*FP*):   Encoding of a signed number expressed
                                    as a mantissa and a signed exponent.
                                    The representation is not significant for
                                    this investigation.

BOOLEAN (*BOOL*):   Encoding of boolean TRUE and FALSE.
                                    Again, the actual representation is of lit-
                                    tle significance.

CODEBLOCK (*CB*):   A pointer to a CODEBLOCK in program
                                    memory. For the sake of the present dis-
                                    cussion, a codeblock can be though of as
                                    an atomic collection of machine instruc-
                                    tions, *i.e.*, a compiled unit. A more com-
                                    plete definition of codeblocks and their
                                    relationship to user-written procedures is
                                    given in Section 4.1.

I-STRUCTURE DESCRIPTOR (*ISD*):   A pointer to an I-Structure in global I-
                                    Structure storage which also encodes the
                                    bounds of the structure.

I-STRUCTURE ADDRESS (*ISA*):   A pointer to an element in global I-
                                    Structure storage.

INSTRUCTION ADDRESS (*INSTR*):   A pointer to an instruction in a loaded
                                    codeblock.

CLOSURE DESCRIPTOR (*CD*):   An encoding of a codeblock pointer, an in-
                                    teger arity, an integer number of ar-
                                    guments as yet unspecified, and the I-
                                    Structure address of the argument list.

FRAME DESCRIPTOR (*FD*):   A pointer to a frame in frame storage.

ITERATION DESCRIPTOR (*ID*):   A tuple of a program counter, two boolean
                                    flags and three index offsets used to im-

---

[20]In the results presented herein, the only form of autocoercion actually used is for
numbers (integer and floating-point number) and is defined more precisely in [6].

plement the K-bounded loop schema, described in detail in Section 4.3. Format is

`<PC,FLAGS,P,C,N>`

where P, C, and N are the index offsets denoting areas in the frame for the previous, current, and next iterations respectively.

CONTINUATION DESCRIPTOR (*CD*): A tuple containing a pointer to the next instruction to be executed (program counter), a pointer to a frame base, and three index registers. The format is strongly similar to that of an iteration descriptor:

`<PC,FBR,P,C,N>`

The ARITHMETIC pseudo-type (*ARITH*) is used notationally to indicate an *INT*, *FP*, or *BOOL* as will be clear from the context. The ANY pseudo-type (*ANY*) is used notationally to indicate any hardware type. These two meta-types are not meaningful at the hardware level.

Name Spaces. Code is to be compiled, named, and loaded on a per-codeblock basis. No limit is assumed on the size of a codeblock, nor is a limit assumed on the size of program, I-Structure, or frame memories. The register namespace is, however, assumed to be finite and small.

Instruction Set. The instruction set is simple and regular in structure, with orthogonal addressing modes and instruction functions.

The basic addressing modes are

- **IMMEDIATE:** a literal value small enough to be encoded directly in the instruction.

- **REGISTER:** The registers are a small, fixed size array of words which provide no synchronization capability, nor are their values guaranteed to persist across potential suspensions.

- **FRAME DIRECT:** The Frame is a vector of words (slots). Frame size is determined at compile time for each procedure. A procedure may only access its own frame slots. Each slot has several presence bits associated with it. The frame holds the state of an invocation. Frame Direct addressing specifies an offset from the frame base to select a slot. The Frame addressing mode has two important sub-modes:

- **Suspensive:** FETCHing with this mode causes the presence bits to be checked and, if no value is present, the current continuation is suspended as described previously.

- **Nonsticky:** Successful execution of an instruction which has performed a FETCH in nonsticky mode will cause the presence bits to be reset, *i.e.*, to indicate the slot is now empty.

- **FRAME INDEXED:** This mode is identical to Frame Direct mode save that the slot is addressed by adding the specified slot number to the frame base plus one of the three index offsets in the continuation. Suspensive and Nonsticky submodes are available here as well.

Unless otherwise noted, input operand addressing may use immediate, register, frame direct, or frame indexed modes. Output operand addressing may use register, frame direct, or frame indexed modes.

The instruction set being used as the compilation target is intentionally unspectacular with the possible exception of the iteration, forking, and closure support instructions which will be described and justified below[21]. The instruction set has the following notable characteristics:

- Each instruction produces, at most, a single explicit result. Instruction outputs are associated with registers or frame slots within a given execution context. All other "outputs" are viewed as side effects.

- Each instruction is simple enough to be executed in a single cycle, modulo the costs of operand references which are discussed in detail in Section 3.3. There are no long-latency instructions.

---

[21]Given the goal of making cogent comparisons to the TTDA, two instruction set design constraints were assumed. First, the TTDA claims that closures can be represented as objects no bigger than a floating point number. Consequently, closure manipulating instructions are of the same complexity as ADD. Second, resource management instructions represent calls to a manager, the instructions of which are not counted for experimentation purposes. Hence, manager ops (marked with a superscript M) and closure ops (marked with a superscript C) are implemented and counted as single instructions.

Table 3-1: Instruction Set		
Instruction Syntax	Operand Types	Comments
NOT DEST, SRC, etc.	$ARITH \Rightarrow ARITH$	monadic arith / logical
ADD DEST, SRC.0, SRC.1, etc.	$ARITH \times ARITH \Rightarrow ARITH$	dyadic arith / logical / relational
MOVE DEST, SRC	$ANY \Rightarrow ANY$	intra-invocation data movement
MOVR DINDX, SRC.0, SRC.1	$FD \times ANY \times INT \Rightarrow \varnothing$	inter-invocation data movement
LOAD FDEST, SRC.0, SRC.1	$ISD \times INT \Rightarrow ANY$	indexed I-Fetch to a frame slot only
STOR DEST, SRC.0, SRC.1	$ISA \times ANY \Rightarrow BOOL$	unindexed I-Store with signal
IXCC DEST, SRC	$INT \Rightarrow FD$	compute new frame base from current
IXSA DEST, SRC.0, SRC.1	$ISD \times INT \Rightarrow ISA$	compute structure element address
IXID DEST, SRC.0, SRC.1	$ID \times INT \Rightarrow ID$	compute iteration descriptor
STPR SRC	$INT \Rightarrow \varnothing$	set previous iteration offset in AC
STCR SRC	$INT \Rightarrow \varnothing$	set current iteration offset in AC
STNX SRC	$INT \Rightarrow \varnothing$	set next iteration offset in AC
STIM DEST, SRC.0, SRC.1	$ID \times BOOL \Rightarrow ID$	set / reset $IMPT_j$; conditionally queue
STPC DEST, SRC.0, SRC.1	$ID \times INSTR \Rightarrow ID$	set PC and $CNTL_j$; conditionally queue
RST1 SRC	$ANY \Rightarrow \varnothing$	reset frame presence bits
RST2 SRC.0, SRC.1	$ANY \times ANY \Rightarrow \varnothing$	reset frame presence bits
TST1 DEST, SRC	$ANY \Rightarrow BOOL$	test frame presence bits with signal
TST2 DEST, SRC.0, SRC.1	$ANY \times ANY \Rightarrow BOOL$	test frame presence bits with signal
TSTL SRC.0, SRC.1	$ID \times INT \Rightarrow \varnothing$	test loop termination
BR TARGET	$INSTR \Rightarrow \varnothing$	unconditional branch
BRF SRC, TARGET	$BOOL \times INSTR \Rightarrow \varnothing$	branch iff FALSE
BRT SRC, TARGET	$BOOL \times INSTR \Rightarrow \varnothing$	branch iff TRUE
BRNZ SRC, TARGET	$INT \times INSTR \Rightarrow \varnothing$	branch iff $\neq 0$
BRZ SRC, TARGET	$INT \times INSTR \Rightarrow \varnothing$	branch iff $= 0$
CNTN TARGET	$INSTR \Rightarrow \varnothing$	fork a new continuation
CNTT SRC, TARGET	$ANY \times INSTR \Rightarrow \varnothing$	fork a new continuation, test slot
MKIC^M DEST, SRC	$INT \Rightarrow ISD$	allocate a CONS cell of given kind
MKIS^M DEST, SRC.0, SRC.1	$INT \times INT \Rightarrow ISD$	allocate an I-Structure w / bounds
MKIV^M DEST, SRC.0, SRC.1	$INT \times INT \Rightarrow ISD$	allocate a vector w / upper bound and kind
GETC^M DEST, SRC	$CB \Rightarrow FD$	allocate an invocation context
RETC^M DEST, SRC	$FD \Rightarrow BOOL$	deallocate an invocation context
CARR^C DEST, SRC	$CD \Rightarrow INT$	closure's number of arguments remaining
CARI^C DEST, SRC	$CD \Rightarrow INT$	closure's arity
CCBN^C DEST, SRC	$CD \Rightarrow CB$	closure's codeblock identifier
CCHN^C DEST, SRC	$CD \Rightarrow ISD$	closure's argument chain pointer
CNCD^C DEST, SRC.0, SRC.1	$CD \times ISD \Rightarrow CD$	build a new closure
CRDY^C DEST, SRC	$CD \Rightarrow BOOL$	test a closure for application

There are primitive instructions for the usual set of arithmetic and logical operations plus the usual complement of relationals. The **MOVE** opcode encodes all intra-invocation data movement. The **MOVR** (MOVe Remote) opcode is used for procedure linkage, and is the only way one procedure can store into another's frame. There is no sanctioned way for one procedure to directly read from another's frame[22].

Data can be moved between the global I-Structure memory and slots/registers only via the **LOAD** and **STOR** instructions. **LOAD** takes a structure base address (*ISD*) and an offset (*INT*), adds them to produce a structure element address, and forwards this along with the target frame slot address to the appropriate remote memory unit, again, without waiting for the result. The name of the instruction implies that the result must be returned to the frame (as opposed to a register). The reason should be clear — the fetched value will return asynchronously, therefore, all consumers must be able to synchronize. Since registers are both volatile and non-synchronizing, they are unsuitable as targets for a fetch-like operation.

STOR performs no indexing (three-address instruction format limit). The structure element address (*ISA*) and the value are forwarded to the memory. A signal value is produced. This is useful for termination detection as discussed in Sections 4.2 and 4.3.

Indexing for **STOR**s is done explicitly by the **IXSA** (IndeX Structure Address) instruction. The **IXCC** (IndeX Current Context) instruction derives new frame base addresses from the context's frame base address, allowing the construction of sub-frame blocks, *e.g.*, for procedure linkage. **IXID** (IndeX Iteration Descriptor) takes an iteration descriptor and adds a given amount to all three of its index offsets.

Index offsets in the active continuation (AC) are explicitly set by the **STPR** (SeT PRevious iteration), **STCR** (SeT CuRrent iteration), and **STNX** (SeT NeXt iteration) instructions. Iterations are conditionally enabled by use of the **STPC** (SeT Program Counter) and **STIM** (SeT IMport flag) instructions which set flags in the iteration descriptor which, when all true, allow the corresponding iteration to begin. The **TSTL** (TeST Loop termination) instruction tests for termination of an iteration by examining the flags in an iteration descriptor.

---

[22]This has an important implication for the way frame storage can be implemented, in particular, it avoids the coherence problem should it become desirable to cache frame data.

The explicit **TSTN** (TeST 1 or 2 slots) and **RSTN** (ReSeT 1 or 2 slots) instructions are not necessary in that their functions can be synthesized from other instructions. For example, **TST1** is the same as **MOVE**ing a value, using the suspensive sub-addressing mode, to another slot. **RST1** is the same as nonsuspensively **MOVE**ing the contents of a slot, using the non-sticky sub-addressing mode, to a scratch register. However, for the sake of instrumentation, separate instruction codes are used in this study.

The branch-like opcodes do the obvious things, causing the PC in the continuation to be replaced (conditionally or unconditionally, as appropriate). The **CNTN** (CoNTiNue) opcode creates (forks) a new continuation. The corresponding join operation is implemented implicitly through frame slot synchronization. **CNTT** (CoNTinue and Test) is functionally identical to **CNTN** (it is not a conditional fork), but is used as part of an important optimization discussed in Section 4.3.

Allocation of processor and memory resources is viewed as the responsibility of the architecture. However, the compilation target only includes the instructions used to invoke some processor-local facility to request these services. Such instructions are **MKIS** (MaKe I-Structure, the general case of a linearly addressed, 1-dimensional array of slots with arbitrary lower and upper bounds — the instruction returns the base address of the structure), **MKIV** (MaKe I-Vector, the less general case of a I-Structure whose lower bound is always 0), **MKIC** (MaKe I-Cons, the less general case of an I-Vector whose upper bound is always 1), **GETC** (GET Context, which allocates an invocation context somewhere in the machine for a given codeblock and returns the base address of the frame), and **RETC** (RETurn Context, which allows a context's resources to be recycled).

Closures are represented as word-sized objects as in the TTDA [56]. Closure manipulation, therefore, amounts to little more than extraction, composition, and simple arithmetic with short bit strings.

Architectural State. The primitive instructions which allocate and deallocate work do so at the level of codeblocks (defined in Section 4.1); an instance of an invoked codeblock is called an INVOCATION CONTEXT or simply an INVOCATION. A codeblock is a collection of SQ's. The state visible to an executing codeblock (more precisely, to the continuations of its SQ's) includes the slots in the invocation's frame, the general purpose

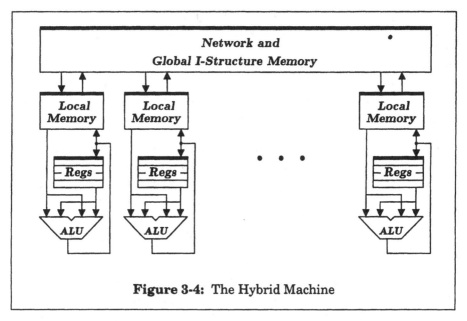

Figure 3-4: The Hybrid Machine

registers, the I-Structure storage, and the descriptor for the current continuation itself. The continuation's descriptor is the root of the accessible state. It points to the next available instruction and to the frame. The frame is entirely local to the invocation.

3.3 EXECUTION MODELS

In this Section, idealized and realistic execution models are presented. At the coarsest level, both the idealized and the realistic machines share a number of common characteristics. In overall structure (Figure 3-4, yet another incarnation of the general model of Figure 1-4) they both follow the dance hall paradigm of a number of identical processors on one side of a routing network, with a number of memory modules on the other side of the network. A processor may send a message either to a memory module or to another processor.

It is assumed that the memory units are actually I-Structure Storage units (per [33]); their structure will not be reiterated here. It is sufficient to assume that the storage units collectively implement a single global address space, and that each accepts requests to LOAD, STORe, or allocate in a pipelined fashion. Further, the service latencies (independent of communication latencies) for allocating or storing are assumed to be bounded. The service latency for loading from an I-Structure is unbounded in that it implies synchronization.

The network's internal structure is of little concern here, save that the transit latency through the network is some reasonably slowly-growing function of the number of inputs (*e.g.*, *log(n)*), that messages can be accepted in a pipelined fashion, and that the acceptance/delivery rate speed-matches both the processor and the structure memory. It is not essential for the sake of this study that the network preserve orderings of messages; however, other higher and lower level concerns may deem it essential (*e.g.*, efficient detection of the completion of all STOR operations from a given invocation).

Instructions may make operand references to a processor's registers or to slots in the processor's large, local data memory. Slots may be read and written imperatively or via the checking of synchronization bits associated with each word. The local memory's synchronizing behavior is as discussed previously. Local memory is referenced relative to a frame base address in the current continuation. Registers are few in number, provide no means for synchronization, and are shared among all continuations. Their contents cannot be considered valid across potentially suspensive instructions.

The Ideal Processor

Before presenting a realizable version of the architecture, it is instructive to consider a slightly more abstract processor which remains true to the compilation model yet hides may engineering-level details of a realizable machine. This IDEALIZED PROCESSOR can be thought of as a von Neumann machine augmented with a synchronizing local memory, and means for manipulating continuations as first class hardware types (Figure 3-5, an embodiment of the concepts in Figure 1-5). This machine has the following attributes:

- Each invocation is assigned its own local memory unit which is only used for that invocation's frame storage. Connected to each such local memory are processors — one for each continuation created by the invocation. Each processor may operate on a single continuation if it is active, or it may sit idle.

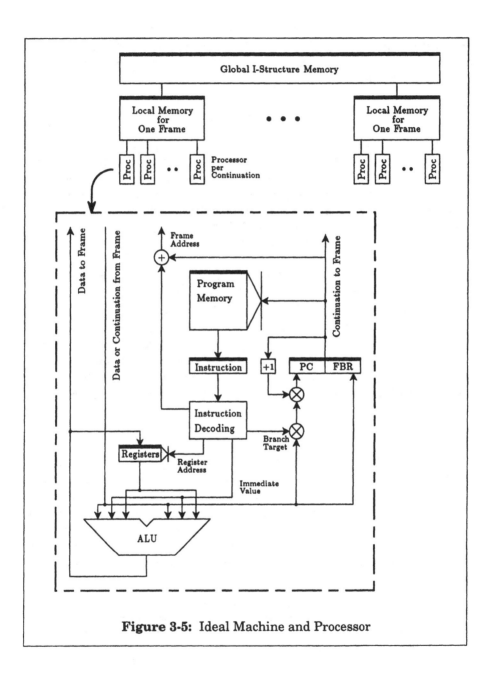

Figure 3-5: Ideal Machine and Processor

- Instructions are executed exactly when they are enabled. Each instruction takes unit execution time and, within any given continuation, instruction i which follows instruction $i-1$ must necessarily execute at some time t_i such that

$$t_i \geq t_{i-1}+1$$

At any given time t, then, as many instructions will execute as there are processors holding active continuations.

- An instruction may access zero, one, or two operands, either in registers or in the local memory (frame slots) without incurring a time penalty. Processors sharing a local memory can access the memory without conflict. Processors may not access any of the other local memories in the machine.

- Performing a synchronizing operand fetch from an empty slot in the local memory causes the affected continuation to be removed from its processor and to be stored in the empty slot. Multiple synchronizing reads against the same slot cause additional continuations to be stored in the same slot. Upon writing a value to a slot containing continuations, the continuations are extracted and returned to their processors.

The idealized model provides a means for studying the effects that architectural and compiler-imposed assumptions have on program execution free of further, hardware-specific constraints. In the next Chapter, experimental results will be presented showing the behavior of a number of programs under the idealized model. These results will provide an interesting comparison to similar results from the TTDA. Also, they will provide a backdrop for studying the behavior of the same programs when executed on a realistic machine model which is discussed next.

The Realistic Processor

The idealized processor represents, in some sense, the best that any hybrid machine can hope to do given the compilation constraints. In this Section, the intractable aspects of the idealized machine are explored in some depth, and architectural directions are identified which will result in a REALISTIC PROCESSOR whose behavior can mimic that of the idealized machine in key ways. The basis of this discussion is a concrete instance of a processor (Figure 3-6). In order to translate its physical characteristics into constraints, a pipeline-level model will be presented and analyzed.

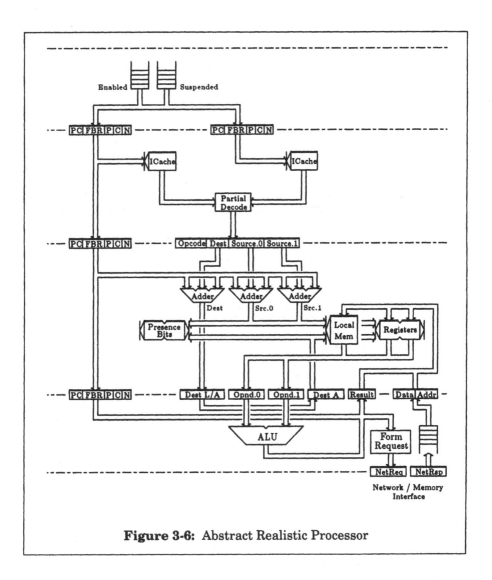

Figure 3-6: Abstract Realistic Processor

Unrealizability. At the most basic level, the idealized model is unrealizable because

- The number of processors cannot be made to scale with the number of continuations. Processor resources must be shared across multiple active continuations. Further, at most one instruction from the set of all those which are logically enabled may execute on any one processor at any given time.

- Local memory ports cannot be made to scale with the number
  of invocations. Like processor resources, local memory must
  be shared.

- Access to the local memory is subject to hard engineering constraints. Unlike the idealized model which permits multiple
  accesses from multiple continuations at any given time, it will
  be difficult to provide access to more than a handful of local
  addresses during a pipeline beat.

- Using local slots to hold suspended continuations is constrained by the size of the slot: at most a single continuation
  can be stored into a slot. Hence, queueing of multiple suspensions requires some additional mechanism.

Also, the model of unit instruction execution time is subject to countless
engineering concerns. It is this issue which has made pipelining such a
popular implementation technique. By this method, the rate of dispatching instructions can be uncoupled from the total execution time of any
given instruction. The difficulty in pipelining a processor arises when
there are inter-dependences between instructions in the pipe.

The model presented in the following Sections is claimed to be realizable.
Instructions are dispatched into a rather shallow pipeline. This Section
briefly examines the hazards of trying to use a pipelined organization to
mimic the behavior of the idealized machine.

At each time step, the ideal model will execute all and only those instructions which are enabled. This implies a means for identifying the set of
enabled continuations and the corresponding set of enabled instructions.
The former problem is easy to deal with in a pipelined machine — continuations are always sorted by their state, specifically, enabled continuations reside exclusively in their own queue or set of queues. The latter
problem is also relatively easy to deal with in a pipelined machine. The
PC in each enabled continuation denotes the instruction to be executed
next. Given sufficient instruction memory bandwidth, all such instructions can logically be fetched in parallel. The hard problem is to know
which of these instructions are actually executable.

In a dataflow machine, construction of the set of enabled instructions is
done automatically by the waiting-matching hardware. In the hybrid
machine, the approach is different — an instruction can be attempted, and

if the synchronization constraints are not met, the instruction is aborted. Efficient means are available for preventing busy-waiting (*viz.*, storage of such suspended continuations in the frame slot which caused the synchronization fault), but in a non-ideal setting, the cost of the faulted instruction cannot be ignored. Moreover, in a real pipeline, several instruction dispatch cycles may pass between the time that a potentially suspensive instruction is initiated until it can be determined that the instruction will actually suspend. Careless dispatching of logical successor instructions behind a potentially suspensive one can result in the flushing of not one, but many instructions depending on the pipe depth. The result on performance may be disastrous.

Given this, consider a method for approximating ideal behavior: means are provided for pre-fetching a subset of the enabled instructions. At each time step, the instruction dispatcher may examine the pre-fetched instructions and choose between them to optimize the behavior of the pipeline. How does the dispatcher make such a decision?

Instructions are to be dispatched so as to keep the pipeline full of useful work. Non-useful work includes execution of NOPs (*i.e.*, pipeline bubbles) and instructions which suspend. Optimal dispatching of instructions is impossible without foreknowledge of which instructions in the set will suspend. However, simple decoding of instructions allows the dispatcher to at least know if the instruction cannot suspend (*e.g.*, those which only reference registers or which make nonsuspensive references to frame memory) or if it might possibly suspend. The strategy presented below builds on this observation, attempting to dispatch instructions from a single SQ instance until an instruction is encountered which might possibly suspend. Dispatching from that SQ instance is deferred long enough to obviate the purging of multiple instructions on the occasion of a fault. During this interval, inter-SQ parallelism is exploited by dispatching instructions from another SQ instance. The number of such pre-fetched instructions is directly related to the number of stages between the dispatching stage and the fault-detecting stage.

Pipeline Overview. The pipeline is synchronous, with registers serving as inter-stage interfaces. In the Figures, registers are depicted as short rectangular boxes with a heavy top-bar (symbolizing an element with state). Stage boundaries are further emphasized with dashed lines. At

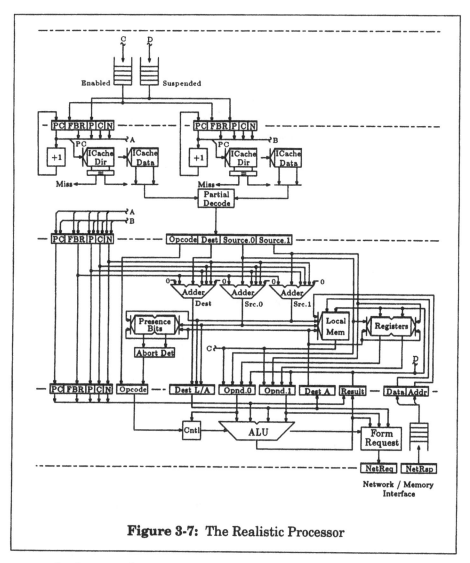

Figure 3-7: The Realistic Processor

every pipe beat, each stage stores its current outputs into the appropriate interface registers (see Figures 3-6 and 3-7).

The first pipeline stage is quite simple (Figure 3-8). Continuations are fetched on demand from the second pipeline stage and are loaded into registers at the interface. The ENABLED CONTINUATION QUEUE holds those continuations which are in the enabled state, while the SUSPENDED

CONTINUATION QUEUE holds continuations which are waiting on slots which already contain a suspended continuation.

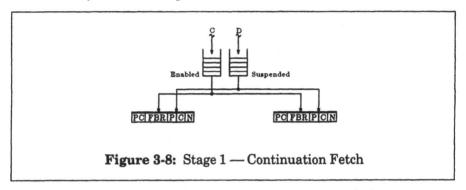

Figure 3-8: Stage 1 — Continuation Fetch

Continuations are fetched from the enabled queue when it is nonempty. Only when the enabled queue is drained is work fetched from the suspended queue. This scheme was borrowed from the Manchester Dataflow project. It is not ideal, but it is simple.

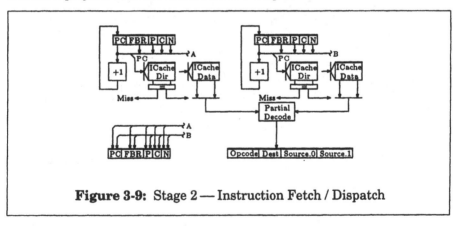

Figure 3-9: Stage 2 — Instruction Fetch / Dispatch

The instruction dispatching logic (Figure 3-9) for the realistic machine is inherently simple. Using two candidate continuations, two such enabled instructions can be considered and the "better" one dispatched at each time step. At any given time, one of the continuations will be called ACTIVE, the other PASSIVE. During each pipe beat, the PC's in each continuation are extracted and are dereferenced through separate instruction caches in order to produce two candidate instructions[23]. The instructions are analyzed according to the following rule[24]:

Algorithm 3-6:

IF the active continuation causes a CACHE MISS,
  THEN Refill the active cache.
    IF the passive continuation causes a CACHE MISS,
      THEN Refill the passive cache.
      Restart { Pipeline Bubble }.
    ELSE Dispatch the passive instruction[25].
      IF the passive instruction is a **TERMINATE**
        THEN Signal to refill the interface register.
      ELSE IF the passive instruction is neither
          SUSPENSIVE nor a BRANCH
          THEN Exchange the sense of active and passive.
  ELSE Dispatch the active instruction.
    IF the active instruction is a **TERMINATE**
      THEN Signal to refill the interface register.
      Exchange the sense of active and passive.
    ELSE IF the active instruction is either SUSPENSIVE or
        a BRANCH[26]
        THEN Exchange the sense of active and passive.

Dispatching means that the interface registers to the third pipeline stage are to be loaded with the selected instruction and its corresponding con-

---

[23]Implementing this function with two caches is simpler than a single, dual-ported cache, but the performance is likely to be inferior. Because any continuation may be assigned to either interface register as it goes through cycles of suspension and resumption, the two caches would tend toward the same contents. By combining the storage, duplicate entries could be avoided and cache misses could be reduced.

[24]It is assumed that **TERMINATE** instructions are not separately encoded but rather that the SQ termination condition is indicated as an opcode modifier for every instruction.

[25]This algorithm relies on there being two banks of registers, active and passive, corresponding to the active and passive continuations. This level of sophistication is not strictly necessary. In fact, the realistic emulator used to evaluate this architecture does not interleave continuations in this way. The performance penalty is program dependent, and the option to interleave at this level is left as an engineering decision. The effects on locality are not well understood.

[26]Interleaving on BRANCH instructions forces the compiler to treat them as potentially suspensive.

tinuation (Figure 3-7). The continuation so loaded contains the PC point-
ing to the selected instruction, not its successor. This PC must be carried
forward in the event that the instruction suspends.

By this method, instructions are dispatched from the active continuation
until termination, dispatching of a suspensive instruction, cache miss, or
branching. In the case of branching, having another continuation on "hot
standby" is a generalization of the delayed branch paradigm in that low-
level parallelism is used to mask the effects of instruction fetch latency.
The difference here, of course, is that the method is dynamic. The compiler need not know precisely how long an instruction prefetch might take.
Moreover, unlike the delayed branch technique, a broader range of candidate instructions may be used to fill in the gap between a branch and
the next sequential instruction, such as instructions from disparate Sections of the program or even other branch instructions[27].

For straight-line, non-suspensive code, instructions will dispatch sequentially, with von Neumann like locality. For code with interspersed unconditional branches, two separate continuations will tend to swap the
processor between them — one will compute while the other resolves a
branch. Assuming that cache resolution takes about the same amount of
time as branch resolution, this behavior will also be observed in the
presence of cache faults. Only when synchronization faults occur will this
behavior change. Thus, known-short latencies are masked by parallelism
without significantly degrading operand locality, and other latencies are
masked by parallelism with the cost in terms of lost locality being, to first
order, proportional to the time spent waiting for synchronization.

---

[27]This kind of parallelism and synchronization can also be used to mask the instruction fetch latency of conditional branches, but the mechanism is necessarily more complex. One approach is to dedicate additional instruction memory bandwidth to parallel
exploration of conditional branch targets as in the IBM 370/168 and its descendants.
Another, less expensive technique is to refine the notion of suspension. In general,
suspension due to a dynamic dependence across SQ's may take unbounded time to
resolve. The situation in the case of of the conditional branch is very different. The
dependence upon the conditional test will always be resolved within a pipe beat or two
of successful operand fetch. For this reason, it is worth considering removing the continuation from the active register upon dispatching a conditional branch. If the boolean
operand is not available, a normal suspension will occur. If the operand is available,
the continuation can be reinserted in the enabled queue (LIFO, perhaps) or into a new
queue which has higher priority than the enabled queue, once the correct PC has been
determined. Giving preferred status to this continuation assures that the presence of
conditional branches does not adversely affect locality.

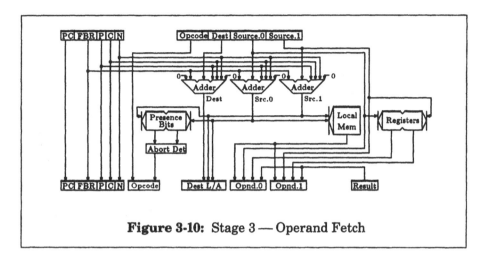

Figure 3-10: Stage 3 — Operand Fetch

The operand fetching stage (Figure 3-10) takes a continuation and an instruction, decodes the addressing modes, and fetches the operands (Opnd.0 and Opnd.1 in the Figure). Each instruction has three fields for operand specification named Dest, Source.0, and Source.1. Within each operand specifier is an addressing mode field and a value field. Section 3.2 describes the addressing modes. These modes select from among the different possible inputs to an operand register:

- **Immediate:** The value is found in the corresponding operand specifier, *i.e.*, an immediate for Opnd.0 would be found in the value field of Source.0.

- **Register:** The value is found in the register file at the offset given in the operand specifier.

- **Frame Direct:** The value is found in the local memory at the offset given by adding the continuation's FBR to the offset given in the operand specifier.

- **Frame Indirect:** The value is found in the local memory at the offset given by adding the continuation's FBR and index register (P, C, or N in the Figure) to the offset given in the operand specifier.

Computation of the destination address is also done at this stage. The result, which specifies either a register or a local memory slot, is stored into the Dest L/A (destination literal/address) interface register. This may involve either passing the Dest field directly from the instruction (in the case of a register or literal) or modifying it by adding the FBR and possibly an index register[28].

If either source specifier indicates a synchronizing reference, the corresponding presence bits are tested. If a synchronization failure occurs (*i.e.*, a required frame slot is empty), an abort is signalled by transforming the instruction into a command to suspend. Subsequent processing will ignore the operand registers and will cause the continuation to be stored into the faulting frame slot. The address of this slot is stored in the Dest L/A register in lieu of the actual destination address.

A special case of source addressing occurs when the destination address of the immediately preceding instruction is the same as one of the source addresses in the current instruction (the case of a sequential dependence). In this case, synchronization testing and operand fetching may be ignored, and the previous instruction's result may be used directly as an input operand, *i.e.*, via bypassing, and obviates pipe bubbles which would otherwise occur while fetching a recently-computed result which has not yet been stored away.

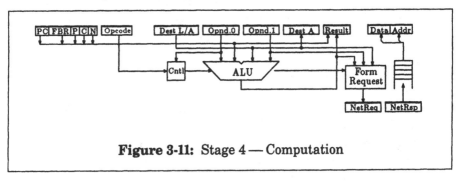

Figure 3-11: Stage 4 — Computation

The computation Section of the pipeline (Figure 3-11) seems anticlimactic when compared to the previous pipeline stages. In this Section, a new result is computed and/or a network request (*e.g.*, to initiate a **LOAD**, **STOR**,

---

[28]Having a "literal" as a destination means only that the destination field contains a literal value to be used in further computing the destination target for the instruction. An important application of this option occurs in the **MOVR** instruction, described below.

or **MOVR**) is formulated. In parallel, the destination address is copied to the corresponding interface register. The ALU and Form Request units are conditioned on the Opcode which may indicate a suspension — if so, the value loaded into the Result register is the continuation. The destination address will have been set to denote the slot causing the synchronization fault. All inbound network traffic is queued (FIFO) in this stage and presented to the local memory via an interface register.

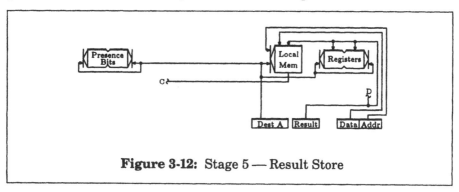

Figure 3-12: Stage 5 — Result Store

As the last phase of instruction execution, the result is stored (Figure 3-12). The Dest A (destination address) register indicates the target as local memory or the register array, and specifies the offset. The value to be stored is found in the Result register. Stores to the register array are straightforward, while stores to the local memory require checking and updating of presence bits:

Algorithm 3-7:

IF presence bits indicate the slot currently
  holds a waiting continuation
  THEN IF a continuation is being written
      THEN Send the new continuation to the
        Suspended queue ("D").
      ELSE Extract the stored Continuation
      Send it to the Enabled queue ("C")
      Write the value.
      Set the presence bits to **Written**.
  ELSE IF a continuation is being written
      THEN Write the continuation.
      Set the presence bits to **Waiting**.
      ELSE Write the value.
        Set the presence bits to **Written**.

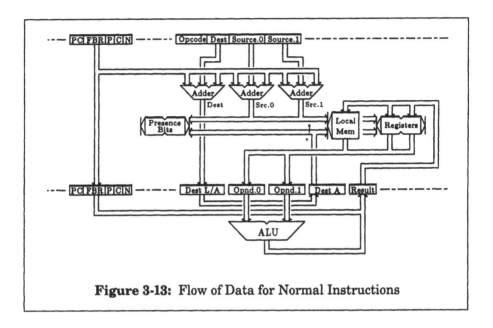

Figure 3-13: Flow of Data for Normal Instructions

Network responses are stored in the frame just as are non-continuations. They extract a waiting continuation and queue it, if there is one, and they set the presence bits to **Written**.

Sequencing and Interlock. Attention now shifts to the temporal behavior of the pipeline. First, several instruction examples are given to show how various resources are used. Then, several resource contention problems are investigated, and solutions are proposed.

The majority of instructions (*e.g.*, arithmetic, logical, closure) execute by the paradigm of performing synchronized or unsynchronized operand fetch, computing a new value, and storing of that value. Selection of the next instruction to be executed depends on the success of operand fetching, as described above, but the normal case will choose the next sequential instruction. The flow of data for this class of instructions is shown in Figure 3-13. In this case, operands may reside in the frame or in registers. Literal operands are also permitted but the data path is not shown in the Figure (see Figure 3-7 for details). Presence bits are tested for any synchronizing reference to the frame, and synchronization failure causes the instruction to be aborted as described above. These instructions produce no network messages.

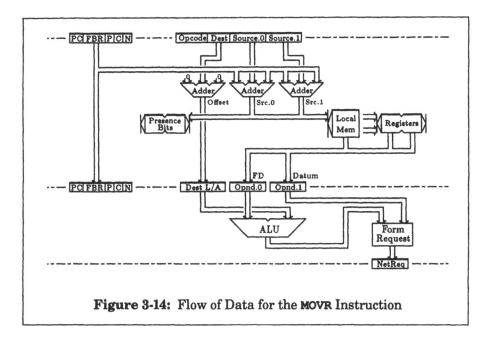

Figure 3-14: Flow of Data for the MOVR Instruction

MOVR, the sole instruction for moving a datum from one execution context directly to another, is shown in Figure 3-14. Operand Src.0 will be the frame descriptor of the destination frame, and the Dest field will contain an immediate index into that frame. Operand Src.1 will be the datum to send. Hence, only the frame descriptor and the datum may cause a synchronization event. The main ALU adds the immediate index to the frame descriptor, and the Form Request unit takes this result and the datum, and forms a network request packet. Although not shown in the Figure, it is possible for MOVR to suspend just as a normal instruction would. In this case, the continuation would be stored as shown in Figure 3-13. MOVR initiates a split transaction and does not block the pipeline awaiting the remote store. It is possible to optimize this in the case that the destination frame resides on the same processor — the result can be stored as in a MOVE instruction.

LOAD takes an *ISD* and an index, computes an *ISA* by adding the index to the base address in the *ISD*, computes the frame address into which the result is to be stored, and forms a network request made up of the *ISA* and the *FD*. The flow is shown in Figure 3-15. Like MOVR, LOAD initiates a split transaction operation. Unlike MOVR, the result can only return to the

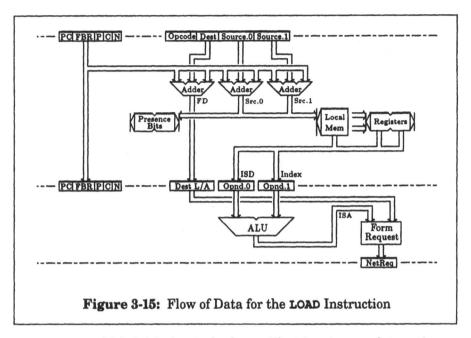

Figure 3-15: Flow of Data for the LOAD Instruction

processor on which initiation took place. That is, at some future time a network response will arrive carrying the requested datum, and bearing the *FD* computed by the MOVR.

STOR takes an *ISA* and a datum, constructs a network request to store the datum at the indicated address, and generates a signal (see Figure 3-16). Logically, this operation produces no local result. The signal is necessitated for termination detection as in the TTDA, but subject to the optimizations discussed in Section 4.3, *i.e.*, that the signal need only be tested across SQ boundaries. There are many other instructions in the instruction set which logically produce no local result but which do not generate a signal. Signal generation is only necessary to preserve the connectedness of the program graph — in the case of these other instructions, they are consistently used in such a way that the connectedness is guaranteed by other means. STOR implements the second half of the I-STORE program graph instruction and necessarily must generate a signal. See Section 4.3.

As mentioned previously, the TSTN instructions are simply special codings of instructions which synchronize on one or two operands and which

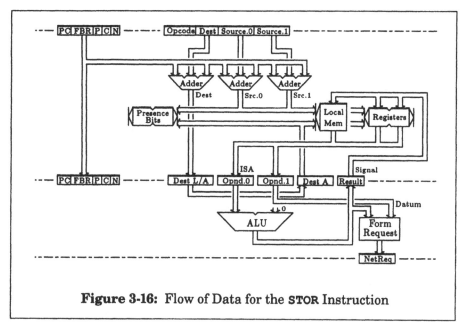

Figure 3-16: Flow of Data for the **STOR** Instruction

simply produce a dummy result (such coding is used for instrumentation purposes only). **RSTN** is similar in that is a special coding of a nonsticky **MOVE** to a null destination. These instructions reset the presence bits for one or two frame slots. The data flow is straightforward and is shown in Figure 3-17. Neither a local result nor a network request is produced.

The **BRXX** instruction executions fall into the following categories:

- **Synchronization Failure:** The predicate argument is read

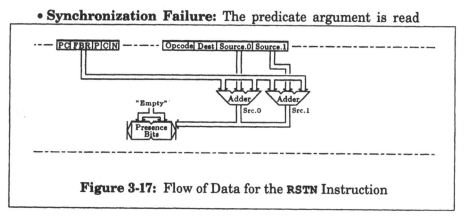

Figure 3-17: Flow of Data for the **RSTN** Instruction

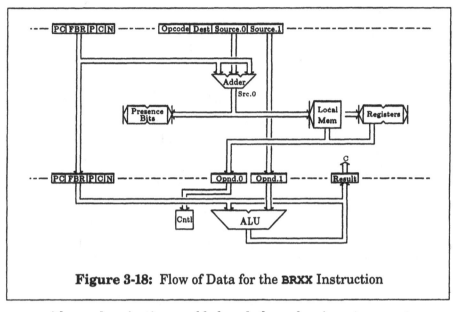

Figure 3-18: Flow of Data for the **BRXX** Instruction

with synchronization enabled and the value is not present. This results in a standard suspension as per the normal case. The unmodified continuation is stored into the predicate slot.

- **False Predicate:** The predicate argument is read and the resulting test computes **FALSE**. The PC is incremented in the main ALU, and the continuation is re-queued.

- **True Predicate:** The predicate argument is read and the resulting test computes **TRUE**. The instruction-specified target, interpreted as a relative offset, is added to the PC in the main ALU and the resulting continuation is re-queued. This case is shown in Figure 3-18.

The **CNTX** opcodes are similar. **CNTN** fabricates a copy of the existing continuation in the main ALU by adding the relative target to the current PC, and then queueing it as an enabled continuation (without suspending the current continuation). **CNTT** provides a slight variant in that it tests the given slot in conjunction with building a new continuation. If the slot has not been written to, the new continuation is stored directly into it. Otherwise, the new continuation is queued. The intention is to avoid wasting cycles scheduling a continuation which will predictably suspend.

To support multiple, concurrent iterations, each continuation contains three index registers (P, C, and N, for *previous iteration, current iteration,* and *next iteration,* respectively) which may be used via the frame indexed operand addressing mode. Each iteration has an area of the frame set aside for it (the format is shown in Section 4.3), and the first slot is reserved for an iteration descriptor whose structure is identical to that of a continuation, save the replacement of the frame base register in the continuation with a set of boolean flags. These flags indicate the necessary iteration enabling conditions described in Section 4.3, specifically, that the $i-1^{st}$ iteration's predicate has computed a **TRUE** predicate (CNTL_{i-1}) and that the $i-K+1^{st}$ iteration has ended (IMPT_{i-K+1}). These iteration descriptors are precomputed and loaded into the 0th slots of each iteration subframe, and are used in the construction of continuations when iterations become enabled.

The **MKIC, MKIS, MKIV, GETC,** and **RETC** instructions provide linkage to local managers (they may be thought of as supervisor calls). The opcode implicitly specifies a code entry point at some fixed address in program memory, and the instruction denotes the arguments to be passed and the destination target. No state-saving takes place, and it is a matter of choice as to whether these instructions are always considered to be suspensive (independent of addressing modes). It is believable that certain managers could be written as nonsuspensive routines and, therefore, that the manager-calling instruction could be treated as such. In the general case, however, the manager-calling instruction is an abstraction of an arbitrary code sequence underneath. It is safe for the compiler to view manager calls as suspensive (meaning that the compiler does not rely on the contents of registers across the call).

Because manager calls represent an implicit break in the flow of control, the instruction dispatcher will have to forestall the dispatching of other instructions from the same continuation by treating a manager call as **BRANCH**-like.

The **STNX, STCR,** and **STPR** instructions are monadic and have the side effect of inserting the next, current, and previous iteration indices, respectively, into the current continuation. The **IXID** instruction behaves as a normal, dyadic instruction, and has the effect of incrementing all three in-

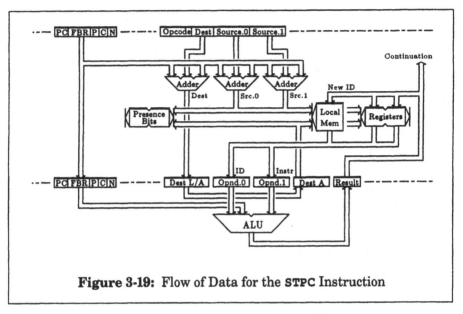

Figure 3-19: Flow of Data for the **STPC** Instruction

dices in an iteration descriptor by the same amount[29]. **TSTL** is dyadic and is used to detect termination of the iteration clean-up code as a necessary precondition to exiting a **LOOP**.

STPC and **STIM** are slightly more complex. **STPC** sets the PC field of the iteration descriptor and also asserts the $CNTL_i$ condition, *i.e.*, it sets the flag. **STIM** sets or resets $IMPT_i$. In addition, both of these instructions check the flags to see if the corresponding iteration has become enabled. If so, a continuation is fabricated by substituting the current FBR from the current continuation into the iteration descriptor, thus creating a new continuation. This continuation is queued, and the iteration descriptor with both flags reset is stored. If instead the iteration is not yet enabled, the iteration descriptor is simply stored; no continuation is fabricated. The flow is shown in Figure 3-19.

With this understanding of the basic operation of each instruction, attention now turns to the effects of instruction sequences, *e.g.*, network loading, pipeline balance, and resource overcommitment.

---

[29]It is a straightforward matter to logically partition a wide ALU/adder into several smaller ALU's/adders by appropriate gating in the carry lookahead logic, thereby permitting **IXID** to execute three additions in a single cycle.

There is an important asymmetry between the ALU's path to the local memory and the network's path. Given ongoing contention between these two paths for the local memory, it is possible to consider suspending the ALU path (and thereby holding up the entire pipe) in order to resolve the conflict. Choosing instead to suspend the network path admits the possibility of deadlock. This does not mean, however, that a given network response must take absolute priority over all instruction results in competing for access to the local memory. Rather, the last pipe stage is free to hold the store for a network response in abeyance until the execution of an instruction which produces no local result subject to the constraint that the network response queue does not overfill. At the system level,

- The number of network responses is equal to the sum of **LOAD** and non-local **MOVR** instructions.

- The number of time-slots for handling network responses is the sum of instructions producing no local result, specifically, **LOAD, RSTN, BRXX, CNTX**, and non-local **MOVR**.

It is a matter for further analysis to determine the relationship between the necessary queue size as a function of the statistics of **RSTN, BRXX,** and **CNTX** instructions. The difficult issue will, of course, be locally significant variations from average numbers, causing response queues to fill. In order to guarantee that a processor can always accept network responses, queue filling should be a sufficient condition for pipeline suspension to allow responses to be stored.

Despite the machine's appearance as a simple five-stage pipeline, in reality the third and fifth stages share key resources, *viz.*, the register file, the presence bits, and the frame store. In any one pipe beat, two operands will be fetched for the current instruction, one result will be stored for a preceding instruction and, if that result is destined for a frame slot containing a continuation, the continuation must be fetched. Building a small register file which supports two reads and one write in a pipe beat is entirely reasonable. Presence bits are harder to handle both because there are more of them (a few bits per local memory slot) and because of the need for three reads instead of two. The hardest problem, however, is implementing three reads and one write for the local memory.

One approach, used in the IBM 43xx and in other machines, is to observe that the address for the write operation is available at the very beginning

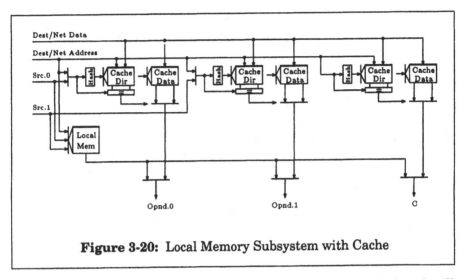

Figure 3-20: Local Memory Subsystem with Cache

of each pipe beat, while the read addresses must be computed and will therefore not be available until later in the cycle. There is, therefore, an opportunity to reduce the number of simultaneous accesses by performing one access (either reading a stored continuation or writing a new value) prior to performing the operand fetches. With a memory whose cycle time is half a pipe beat, the requirement can be relaxed to two reads and one write instead of three and one. Building a two-read, one-write memory then requires simply duplicating the memory with the appropriate cycle time constraints.

This is both wasteful and impractical for large memories. Another tack is simply to suspend pipeline operations until all local memory operations can be resolved. Thus, if the memory runs at the rate of one access (read or write) per minimum pipe beat, three references will cause the introduction of two additional bubble cycles downstream in the pipe. This technique can be practical, however, when instruction statistics indicate an average of less than one frame access per instruction (*e.g.*, register-intensive sequential execution). An extreme instance of this is to impose constraints on the compiler which explicitly limit the number of local memory references as a function of time.

A better solution is to exploit the locality that the machine works so hard to preserve. By introducing a tri-ported, store-through operand cache in parallel with the local memory, it is possible in principle to significantly reduce the number of read requests which the local memory must satisfy to the point where it only handles writes (one per beat). Such a cache subsystem is depicted in Figure 3-20.

Possibly the best approach would be to use a pipelined local memory subsystem [37] whose pipe beat is significantly faster than that of the processor. This approach is not investigated here. Another technique not studied is to avoid storing continuations in frame slots entirely and instead to use the Suspended queue to contain all suspended continuations. This has the advantage of reducing the absolute worst-case requirements on the frame to two reads and one write per cycle. The potentially deleterious effects on locality and exposed parallelism of this technique are not well understood.

Exploiting Parallelism. It is worth reviewing how all these mechanisms allow the exploitation of the various forms of parallelism outlined in Section 2.3.

- Expression-level parallelism is best used for masking latency by keeping the pipeline full, as in a von Neumann machine. The sequential dispatching of instructions from a given instance of a given SQ allows exactly this behavior. Fast context switching between SQ instances (continuation exchange at the instruction dispatch stage) further allows low-level parallelism to be used in masking latency. The manner of using registers between suspensive instructions allows high-speed, multiport access to data while keeping the cost of context switching very low.

- Inner-loop parallelism is supported by representing each loop as a codeblock and providing efficient means for sending data between codeblocks. The mechanisms here are the **GETC/RETC** instructions for allocating and deallocating contexts, the **MOVR** instruction for argument / result transfer, and the fine-grained synchronization on frame slots which can be used to support nonstrict invocations (at the same level is procedure call parallelism — the same mechanisms can be used).

- Outer-loop inter-iteration parallelism is supported by representing the storage for an iteration explicitly, and allowing multiple storage areas to be named and addressed. The mechanisms provided include the continuation-specific index registers, iteration descriptors, and instructions for manipulating them (setting, testing, and conditionally scheduling).

Modeling Latency. For the purposes of performing the emulation study presented in Chapter 5, some assumptions must be made regarding latencies. In fact, transit latency is left as a degree of freedom and, in the experiments, latency will be varied to measure the latency-tolerating effectiveness of the model. It will be assumed throughout, however, that instruction service latency (the pipe beat) is unity, and that the I-Structure storage processor is similarly pipelined.

Handling Finite Resources. Questions of how this architecture manages its finite resources are beyond the scope of the present work. It is claimed that solutions applicable to machines such as the TTDA are equally applicable here because of the following relevant architectural similarities:

- Demand for context-specific storage is not only bounded, but is known *a priori*. Each codeblock carries with it a record of the number of frame slots necessary for invocation (the actual value is a function of K, the invocation-time parameter which controls loop unfolding). It is a purely local decision to determine if a given processor has sufficient space to invoke a given codeblock with a given value of K.

- Register requirements are likewise bounded at compile time.

- Invocation requests are processor-nonspecific. The response to a **GETC** is a frame descriptor which identifies both the frame base address and the processor in which the frame resides. Thus, if a local manager cannot satisfy a **GETC** request based on local information, the request can be handled by any other processor in the machine. The question of how best to to make such decisions is an open problem for this machine, the TTDA, Monsoon [46], and other similar machines.

- The queue overflow problem, related to the codeblock invocation problem, is analogous to the same problem on machines like the TTDA and Monsoon. One minor difference is that those machines queue continuations for single instructions, while the hybrid machine queues continuations for SQ's. That is, because expression-level parallelism is represented by properly-ordered sequential code in the hybrid model, there will necessarily be fewer extant continuations at any given time during program execution than in a machine supporting single-instruction parallelism. This has some engineering, but little theoretical, significance.

- As in the TTDA and Monsoon, and unlike machines such as MASA [29, 32, 53], there is no notion of migrating or transporting a "task" and its state to another processor after invocation.

3.4 SUMMARY

Basic changes to traditional architecture are necessary for dealing with latency and synchronization. One such change is that the execution time for any given instruction must be independent of latency (giving rise to split transactions). A second change is that synchronization mandates hardware support: each synchronization event requires a unique name as does each communicating code fragment. This synchronization name space is necessarily large, and name management must be efficient. To this end, a compiler should generate code which calls for synchronization when and only when it is necessary. A natural approach is to extend instruction sets to express the concepts of both implicit and explicit synchronization. Such an instruction set, which captures the notions of bounded instruction execution time, a large synchronization name space, and means of trading off between explicit and implicit synchronization is called a Parallel Machine Language.

A compilation target has been defined which satisfies these requirements. The instruction set is not unlike that of a von Neumann machine but has been explicitly augmented with synchronization bits on each local memory slot, addressing modes to support synchronization, rapid context switching, instructions for dynamic resource allocation, and an execution model which admits concurrent execution of declared sequential code fragments. Ideal and realistic execution models have been developed. Basic engineering concerns regarding realizability have also been addressed. It has been claimed that this architecture is capable of exploiting the same types of parallelism as a dataflow machine, albeit in somewhat different ways. If true, this architecture is demonstrably superior to a von Neumann machine for the purpose of building a scalable, general-purpose parallel computer, and may offer advantages over pure dataflow approaches as well in that it can execute sequential threads efficiently.

Chapter Four

Compiling for the

Hybrid Architecture

This chapter considers the task of transforming dataflow program graphs into partitioned graphs, and thence into PML. Section 4.1 extends the work of Section 1.1 by completing the description of DFPG's. Section 4.2 discusses the issues involved in generating partitioned code from DFPG's. Section 4.3 presents the design of a suitable code generator.

4.1 DFPG REVISITED

The generation of PML for a program begins with analysis of its DFPG. The analysis seeks to split a monolithic graph into smaller components both to make the graphs more manageable and to exploit static scheduling. First, the remainder of the DFPG instruction set must be described.

DFPG Instructions

On occasion, it is necessary for the compiler to represent explicit copying of a value. In other situations, it is necessary to control the visibility of a value until some condition has been satisfied (historically called GATING). Both of these operations are handled by the **IDENTITY** instruction.

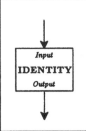

IDENTITY *Instructions*

These produce an output token which is a copy of the first input token. In practice, Identity instructions may have additional trigger inputs which are necessary for firing but which otherwise take no part in the production of the output token. They produce no side effects.

The general case of conditional execution is expressed by the **IF** encapsulator:

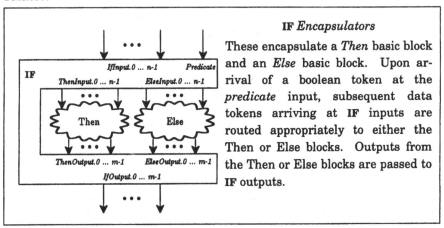

IF *Encapsulators*

These encapsulate a *Then* basic block and an *Else* basic block. Upon arrival of a boolean token at the *predicate* input, subsequent data tokens arriving at **IF** inputs are routed appropriately to either the Then or Else blocks. Outputs from the Then or Else blocks are passed to **IF** outputs.

The explicit allocation of I-Structure storage is represented by the **MAKE-I-STRUCTURE** instruction. Several variations of this instruction support particular higher level data types which are implemented with I-Structures.

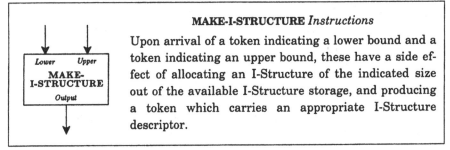

MAKE-I-STRUCTURE *Instructions*

Upon arrival of a token indicating a lower bound and a token indicating an upper bound, these have a side effect of allocating an I-Structure of the indicated size out of the available I-Structure storage, and producing a token which carries an appropriate I-Structure descriptor.

The **MAKE-TUPLE** instructions are similar, but the lower bound is assumed to be zero. Likewise are the **MAKE-CONS** instructions, but both lower and upper bounds are assumed (0 and 1) and produce a descriptor upon receipt of a trigger. **ARRAY** instructions allocate and produce a token describing a multi-dimensional array of I-Structure elements given a set of lower and upper bound tokens as input. **MAKE-STRING** instructions are similar to **MAKE-TUPLE** instructions, but they not only allocate a structure, they also store the characters of the given string into the structure. The **CLOSURE-NCDR** instruction is functionally related, in that it extends a closure's argument chain by allocating a *CONS* cell and then building a new closure using the extended chain.

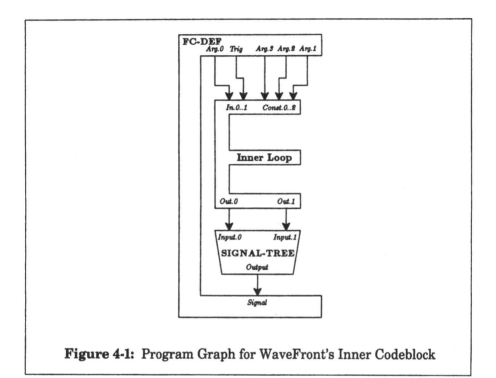

Figure 4-1: Program Graph for WaveFront's Inner Codeblock

Codeblocks

The compilation scheme presumed here translates user procedures into sets of CODEBLOCKS. A codeblock is a partition of a DFPG which meets the following requirements:

- It implements at most a single user procedure.
- It contains at most one non-nested **LOOP**.

In order to satisfy the first condition, individual DFPG's are generated for each user procedure after lambda-lifting [39] internal procedure definitions to top level and replacing all instances of calls to such procedures with partially-applied closures. Such lifted procedures are compiled separately as if they themselves were user procedures.

The second condition is satisfied by first counting the number of outer loops in each procedure. If there is more than one outer loop, the second and subsequent loops are extracted as codeblocks in and of themselves. In their place, a kind of procedure call is substituted. Then, all codeblocks are analyzed for nested loops. As for multiple outer loops, nested loops are extracted as separate codeblocks, and a procedure call is substituted. The procedure calling mechanism which provides the logical glue must preserve nonstrictness, so invocation and partial computation are entirely possible just as they would have been prior to splitting the graph.

Hence, a single user procedure containing internal definitions and multiple, nested loops will be compiled into a number of separate codeblocks. This strategy is not the only one possible, but the rationale for splitting user procedures along these lines does make certain architectural problems, such as allocating dynamic storage and constant areas for loops considerably easier. The interested reader is directed to [56].

Codeblock Encapsulation. An example of the DFPG for an inner loop codeblock is shown in Figure 4-1. The parameter passing mechanism is represented abstractly by the **FASTCALL-DEF** encapsulator for inner codeblocks such as this. Codeblocks for a procedure's top level are enclosed in the related **DEF** encapsulator.

DEF *Encapsulators*

These enclose the bodies of codeblocks, and hide the details of parameter passing and argument chain unpacking. They are implicitly triggered by invocation of the codeblock through an appropriate **APPLY**-like instruction. **DEF** encapsulators have no inputs or outputs on the exterior surface, and enclose only a single basic block called the *Body*. Outputs which feed the body are the codeblock's arguments and a trigger. Inputs are the codeblock's result and a termination signal.

FASTCALL-DEF encapsulators are similar except that they perform no argument chain unpacking and may have multiple result inputs.

Although not shown in the example graph, top level and inner codeblocks are invoked with the **APPLY** and **FASTCALL-APPLY** instructions, respectively.

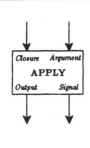

APPLY *Instructions*

These accept a closure token and an argument token. If, given the argument, the arity of the codeblock denoted by the closure is satisfied, the codeblock is applied to the arguments collected in the argument chain along with the argument on the input token. If the arity is not satisfied, a new closure is created which is a copy of the input closure save that the argument chain has been extended with the new argument.

DIRECT-APPLY instructions accept a codeblock descriptor and a set of arguments, applying the codeblock to the arguments. **APPLY-UNSATISFIED** instructions behave like **APPLY** instructions with the exception that it is assumed the arity will not be satisfied by the argument. In all cases, codeblock application is strict in the closure or codeblock descriptor but nonstrict in the arguments. Also, such codeblock application will return at most a single result. **FASTCALL-APPLY** instructions are nearly identical to **DIRECT-APPLY** instructions save that they may return multiple results.

Procedure Linkage. The **DEF**- and **APPLY**-like instructions presume the following skeletal procedure linkage mechanism. Codeblocks may represent top level procedures, *e.g.*, user procedures or lambda-lifted internal definitions, or they may represent inner loops. The procedure linkage conventions are different for the two cases.

Top level codeblocks are represented at the program graph level by a **DEF** encapsulator enclosing the procedure body. The implied protocol between an **APPLY** instruction and the corresponding **DEF** involves

1. Notifying a resource manager to set up a suitable execution environment for an instance of the invoked procedure (**APPLY**).

2. Forwarding of the argument chain and the last argument, when available, to the invoked procedure (**APPLY**).

3. Returning of the result (if there is one) to the invoker (**DEF**).

4. Returning of a termination signal to the invoker (**DEF**).

5. Notifying a resource manager to deallocate the execution environment (**APPLY**).

The **DEF** is responsible for unpacking the argument chain (an I-Structure) then feeding these values, when available, plus a trigger to the body. The same **DEF** is also responsible for fielding invocations where the argument values are sent directly from the invoker, bypassing chain construction and unpacking (this is the **DIRECT-APPLY** variation on procedure invocation).

Internal loop codeblocks are represented at the program graph level by a **FASTCALL-DEF** encapsulator enclosing the codeblock body. The implied protocol between a **FASTCALL-APPLY** instruction and the corresponding **FASTCALL-DEF** involves

1. Notifying a resource manager to set up a suitable execution environment for an instance of the invoked codeblock (**FASTCALL-APPLY**).

2. Forwarding of the arguments, when available, to the invoked codeblock (**FASTCALL-APPLY**).

3. Returning of the results to the invoker (**FASTCALL-DEF**).

4. Returning of a termination signal to the invoker (**FASTCALL-DEF**).

5. Notifying a resource manager to deallocate the execution environment (**FASTCALL-APPLY**).

The major difference is that there is never an argument chain. Arguments are always sent as in **DIRECT-APPLY**. Further, there may be multiple results.

4.2 STRATEGIC ISSUES FOR PARTITIONING

Following the generation of DFPG's and the partitioning into codeblocks, it remains to macroexpand the encapsulators, transliterate the low-level graph instructions to actual machine instructions, partition into SQ's, perform peephole optimization, and assemble. This section investigates the issues of SQ partitioning.

Possible Constraints

Graph partitioning for the PML model may be done in a number of ways. Issues of concern include

- **Maximization of exploitable parallelism:** Poor partitioning can obscure inter-procedural and inter-iteration parallelism. The desire to aggregate instructions does not imply any interest in restricting or limiting useful parallelism — in fact, those cases where instructions may be grouped into SQ's are quite often places where parallelism is exploited in instruction ordering to mask latency.

- **Maximization of run length:** Longer SQ's will ultimately lead to longer intervals between context switches (RUN LENGTH). Coupled with proper runtime support for suspension and resumption, this can lead to increased locality. Run lengths which are long compared to the pipeline depth have a positive effect on shortening critical path time and increasing locality. Short run lengths (frequent instruction aborts due to suspension of a frame reference) tend to bubble the pipeline.

- **Minimization of explicit synchronization:** Each arc which crosses SQ boundaries will require dynamic synchronization. Since synchronization operations are pure overhead[30], it is desirable to minimize them.

- **Deadlock avoidance:** Non-sequentiality and lenience imply that instruction execution order cannot be made independent of program inputs or, said another way, instruction execution order cannot be determined *a priori*. It is necessary to understand where this dynamic ordering behavior will manifest itself in the generated code. Such dynamic ordering must be viewed as a constraint on partitioning since two instructions whose execution order is dynamically determined cannot be statically scheduled in a single SQ.

- **Maximization of machine utilization:** Given a set of costs for instruction execution, context switching, synchronization, and operand access, partitions can be compared on the basis of how well they "keep the pipeline full". This metric is fairly machine specific and is in that sense less general than those previously described but no less important.

---

[30]Coming from a von Neumann uniprocessor mind set where explicit synchronization is virtually unheard of except in situations which require multitasking, it is natural to view synchronization in this way. Coming from the dataflow world where synchronization is unavoidable in every instruction execution and where there is no opportunity to "optimize it out", it is also reasonable to view explicit synchronization instructions as overhead. In a later section, these perspectives are reconciled with the view that explicit synchronization instructions are both necessary and, in some sense, beneficial.

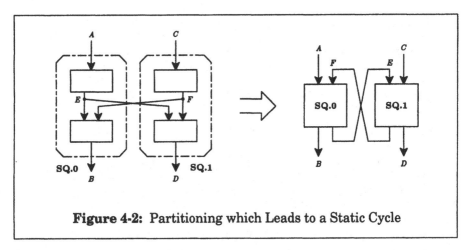

Figure 4-2: Partitioning which Leads to a Static Cycle

Scope

It is not the focus of this work to develop optimal partitioning techniques, but rather, to develop an architecture which can adapt to a spectrum of partitioning strategies per the requirements of the programming language. To that end, this study focuses on development of a safe (deadlock-avoiding) partitioning algorithm for DFPG's generated from Id. This choice is based on three important facts:

1. **Availability of Tools:** At the most pragmatic level, the Id compiler is highly accessible, and provides an excellent vehicle for constructing a prototype hybrid code generator.

2. **Availability of Data:** Id applications have been well-studied on the MIT Tagged-Token Dataflow architecture. By using these same applications, meaningful architectural comparisons can be made.

3. **Difficulty of Partitioning Safely:** Because Id is a lenient language, it does not admit simple, sequential interpretation [58]. In that sense, efficient support for a lenient language will be harder to provide (read: will depend more on efficient dynamic synchronization) than will support for non-lenient languages.

Traub [58] investigates partitioning rules which are provably both safe and efficient. It is his goal to develop the means for maximizing sequential thread size given these constraints. For the purposes of developing the present architecture, the latter constraint has been relaxed, thereby

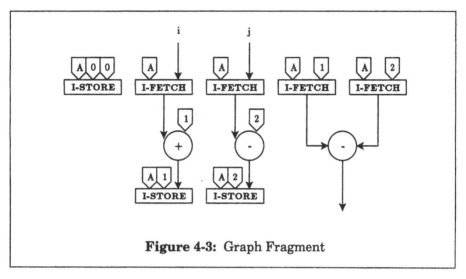

Figure 4-3: Graph Fragment

putting the burden back on the architecture of handling even very small threads efficiently.

Examples

Safe partitioning involves the analysis of both the static structure of a dataflow graph and the dynamic behavior of the graph. This dichotomy leads to two distinct kinds of partitioning problems. Consider first the graph fragment in Figure 4-2. In this example, an acyclic graph is partitioned into two SQ's, each to be executed sequentially. If the partitioned graph is viewed in the abstract with SQ's as the graph nodes, it is curious that the trivial, acyclic graph now has a cycle in it. Because this kind of cycle is a function of the graph's static structure, it is called a STATIC CYCLE.

A very different kind of problem is illustrated with the following Id program fragment:

```
{   a = vector (0,2);
  a[0] = 0;
  a[1] = a[i] + 1;
  a[2] = a[j] - 2;

  in a[1] - a[2] }
```

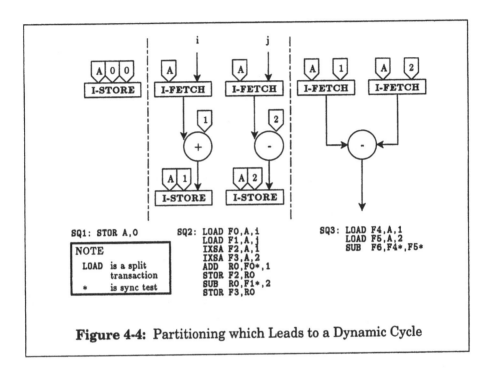

Figure 4-4: Partitioning which Leads to a Dynamic Cycle

and its associated graph[31] in Figure 4-3. **I-FETCH** instructions are assumed to follow split transaction semantics with a non-busy waiting deferred read mechanism [34]. Such a graph would terminate under a dataflow instruction execution rule. However, without exercising some care, partitioning this graph into SQ's can lead to deadlock. Putting all of these instructions into a single partition won't work, nor will a partitioning such as that shown in Figure 4-4. Such partitionings result in code which may never terminate, despite the absence of static cycles.

The problem, of course, is that the actual instruction execution order in the dataflow case depends on the indices used in the structure operations, where no such dependence is allowed in the partitioned case. Figure 4-5 shows two instruction execution orderings which must be possible in any correctly compiled version of this program. These orderings demonstrate the dynamic dependences between **I-STORE**s and **I-FETCH**es. If these

---

[31]The descriptor for vector *A* is depicted as a constant to simplify the drawings. This is done without loss of generality.

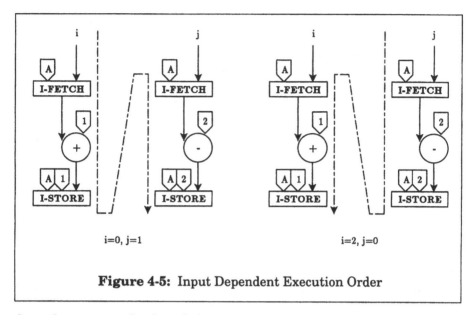

Figure 4-5: Input Dependent Execution Order

dependences were fixed, and if it were possible to determine them at compile time, SQ partitioning to avoid deadlock would be straightforward. Since this is not the case, the problem is one of developing a safe partitioning strategy which is insensitive to the arrangement of dynamic arcs. One approach is to make each partition exactly one instruction long, *i.e.*, the dataflow method. This, of course, is at odds with the desire to exploit static scheduling.

Latency-Directed Partitioning

Extant partitioning algorithms [12, 26] can be classified as depth-first or breadth-first. Depth-first algorithms [12] partition by choosing a path from an input to an output of a graph and making it into an SQ, removing the corresponding instructions from the graph in the process. The algorithm is repeated until no instructions remain unpartitioned. Such partitionings tend to be the best at minimizing critical path time and rely heavily on pipeline bypassing since, by definition, instruction n depends directly on instruction $n-1$. Breadth-first algorithms [26] tend to aggregate instructions which have similar input dependences but only weak mutual dependences.

It is interesting to observe the relationship between the problem of partitioning a dataflow graph and the dynamic "partitioning" of a program which occurs in a multiprogramming environment. Aside from the discretionary kind of context switching which occurs to guarantee fairness among competing tasks, context switching is most often invoked when the running program attempts to synchronize with a long-latency parallel activity, *e.g.*, reading from a disk. Note that it is not in general the initiation of a long latency operation which causes the context switch — it is the attempt to waste time by waiting for the satisfaction of a synchronization constraint. Elaborate mechanisms are designed into such operating systems to allow the waiting task to be put aside and then re-awakened when the event being waited on happens. For such a system to work, the time to switch contexts must be significantly shorter than the time which would, on average, be wasted in waiting.

It is possible to identify the arcs in a dataflow graph which represent long latency operations and the attendant required synchronizations. It is natural to pursue this analogy and to perform SQ partitioning such that no useful work will be postponed simply because a part of the program is waiting for the result of such a long latency operation.

A necessary condition for this kind of analysis is that all such arcs are manifest in the graph, and that none are implicit in the internal behavior of an instruction. Reviewing the dataflow program graph instruction set shows that this condition is violated in several instances:

- **APPLY** and **FASTCALL-APPLY** hide the procedure linkage arcs, in particular, the argument and argument chain arcs which must be synchronized at the called codeblock, and the result and signal arcs which must be synchronized at the caller.

- **DEF** hides the argument chain unpacking (I-Structure references).

The obvious source of long-latency operations is the **I-FETCH** instruction which always implies synchronization prior to use of the fetched value. Less obvious are the **HD**, **TL**, and **TUPLE-FETCH** instructions which are (implicitly) **I-FETCH** instructions. Such outputs of such instructions are

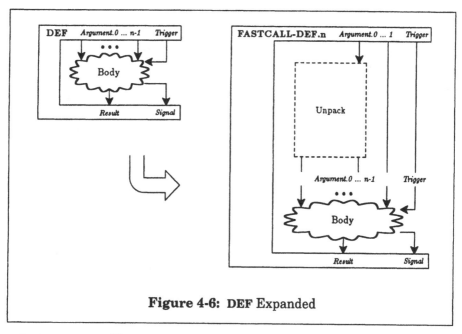

Figure 4-6: DEF Expanded

called **FETCH**-like[32]. See Section 3.2.

Handling of the **DEF** case is straightforward — all **DEF**s are explicitly translated into a simpler form consisting of a set of **HD** and **TL** instructions to unpack the argument chain, plus the body, enclosed by a **FASTCALL-DEF**. By this technique, the embedded **FETCH**-like instructions are made explicit, and the long-latency arcs are likewise represented explicitly.

A similar approach can be taken for **APPLY** instructions. The remaining

---

[32]Instructions which invoke a manager, *e.g.*, **MAKE-I-STRUCTURE**, are potentially long-latency depending upon their implementation which is not implicit in program graph semantics. One can conceive that such instructions package up a manager request and ship it off in the same way that an **I-FETCH** packs and ships its fetch request. In such cases, synchronization would be implied anywhere the instruction's output was used. An equally viable implementation is that the manager will always be resident on the same processor as the executing instruction. In this case, such system calls can be viewed as inline macro expansion, in which case there is no busy waiting. Another perspective is that such instructions consume multiple pipeline cycles, and consume all of the processor resource (productively) in the process. This is the view taken here, therefore, such instructions are not classified as **FETCH**-like.

issue is the handling of the invisible dynamic arcs which link the invoker and the invoked codeblock across the **FASTCALL-APPLY** interface. With **DEF**s rewritten as **FASTCALL-DEF**s, and **APPLY**s rewritten as **FASTCALL-APPLY**s, the synchronizing end of the invoker-to-invoked arcs (arguments and trigger) are simply the output arcs of the **FASTCALL-DEF** (Figure 4-6). Similarly, the synchronizing end of the invoked-to-invoker arcs (results and termination signal) are the output arcs of the **FASTCALL-APPLY**. It is necessary then to consider both **FASTCALL-DEF** and **FASTCALL-APPLY** as **FETCH**-like.

An additional problem arises from the semantics of **APPLY**-like instructions. Upon receipt of the results and the termination signal, these instructions are responsible for deallocating the invoked context's resources. Because this is part of the instruction and because it depends on long-latency arcs, it violates the principle of embedded arcs. For this reason, all instances of **FASTCALL-APPLY** (including those which were originally **APPLY** instructions) are rewritten into component parts which initiate the invocation and separately deallocate it. Doing this introduces two new instructions: **FASTCALL-APPLY-INITIATE** which initiates the procedure invocation, and **SYNCHRONIZING-RETURN-CONTEXT** which frees the invoked context's resources. Rewriting is discussed in detail in Section 4.3.

Summary

Partitioning based on the location of long-latency arcs in the graph is straightforward and has demonstrable advantages over otherwise unguided depth-first or breadth-first strategies. To make any such scheme work, all long-latency arcs must be directly visible at the graph level, and none may be buried in the semantics of a graph instruction. By rewriting certain DFPG instructions into simpler forms, this constraint can be met.

4.3 CODE GENERATOR

With an understanding of the new target model and the structure of DFPG's derived from Id [9], it remains to describe the code generation process. This section presents the details of one possible code generator. A number of interesting problems arise which are characteristic of code generation for parallel machine languages. Solutions to these problems are presented.

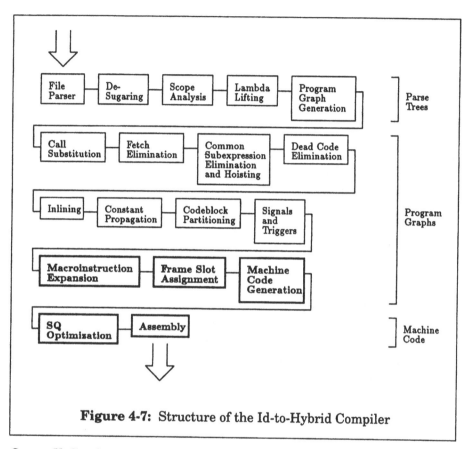

Figure 4-7: Structure of the Id-to-Hybrid Compiler

Overall Goal and Method

A goal of the code generator was to allow existing Id programs to be used as benchmarks for the hybrid architecture. One constraint was not to modify the compiler itself, but rather to use selected modules, intact, to which are added new modules. The overall architecture of the existing Id compiler is described in [56]. Each major phase of the compiler is a separate module with a well-defined input/output interface (*e.g.*, annotated parse tree, annotated dataflow program graph, dataflow machine graph). The modifications consisted of a set of new code generation phases, the first of which maintained the annotated dataflow program graph interface. The resulting compiler (collection of phases) has the structure shown in Figure 4-7. **Boldface** phase names represent those which were added to the existing compiler.

Rather than simply discuss each new phase in turn, it is more illuminating to understand the issues in compiling dataflow program graphs into PML for the given compilation model. In the following sections these issues are raised, and suitable solutions are given. Where appropriate, references are made to the phases which actually perform the work.

Simplifications

DFPG instructions and encapsulators [56] define a rewrite language which can be shown equivalent to Id. In the Id Compiler, program graphs are transliterated to machine graphs through a process of simultaneous macroinstruction expansion and context-free substitution of machine graph instructions for program graph instructions. The DFPG abstraction is useful in that it admits powerful manipulations with relative ease where parse trees would be cumbersome and machine graphs would be too microscopically detailed.

The code generator for the hybrid machine preserves the program graph interface. Input to the code generator is a WELL-FORMED (acyclic compositions of the basic schemata), WELL-CONNECTED (output arcs, called SIGNALS, have been added from instructions which otherwise produce no output, e.g., I-STORE; and input arcs, called TRIGGERS, have been added to instructions which otherwise receive no inputs, e.g., constants) graph.

Code generation begins with macroexpansion of certain DFPG instructions and encapsulators into lower-level program graph equivalents, resulting in a simplified graph. Examples necessitated by instruction semantics for partitioning have already been discussed. The primary purpose in performing further rewrites is to simplify later stages of the code generator by restricting the input language, i.e., reducing the size of the set of possible DFPG instructions. It is particularly important to perform this transformation prior to assigning frame slots — program graphs do not have the property of a one-to-one correspondence between instruction outputs and frame slots. Many required frame slots are "hidden" inside complex program graph instructions. More troublesome, however, is the realization that the number of such hidden slots is a function of the instruction encoding. Hence, this module transforms program graphs into a new kind of graph with a one-to-one correspondence between outputs and slots.

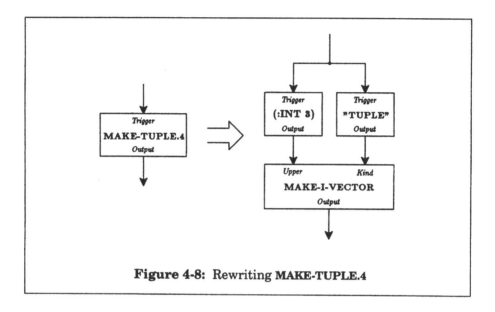

Figure 4-8: Rewriting **MAKE-TUPLE.4**

Macroexpansion is done by context free substitution of a subgraph for a single, complex instruction. Some analysis is performed on instructions to build a proper subgraph. The expansion is recursively applied to the subgraphs until the resulting graph contains only those instructions in the restricted set. In each case, the new subgraph has the same number of inputs and outputs as the old instruction.

Structure Handling Instructions. DFPG instructions for creating strings, tuples, and **CONS**es are rewritten into a simpler form which uses a parameterized **MAKE-I-STRUCTURE** instruction[33] and, as needed, literal constant instructions to represent the I-structure kind and the bounds. This rewriting takes advantage of the ability to embed small literal constants as arguments to any instruction. After this transformation, only one instruction is required to allocate I-structures of any kind. In Figure 4-8, a four-element tuple creation instruction is rewritten into a **MAKE-I-VECTOR** instruction with an implicit lower bound of zero. The up-

---

[33]The operation to allocate an area of the I-Structure storage space can be encoded with a single opcode. However, because of the three-address format of the abstract machine and the desire to collect more fine-grained statistics on storage allocation patterns, three opcodes are used. In this example, **MAKE-I-VECTOR** is an instance of the generic I-Structure creation operation with an implicit lower bound of zero.

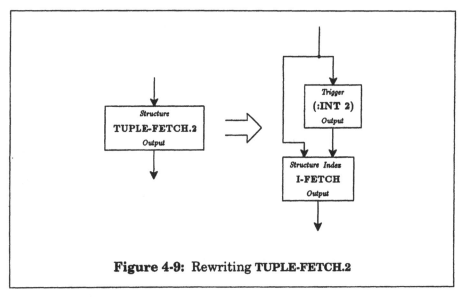

Figure 4-9: Rewriting **TUPLE-FETCH.2**

per bound of three is specified by a literal instruction. The KIND of vector[34] is encoded as an integer.

In a similar fashion, instructions to read or write the elements from strings, tuples, and CONSes are rewritten to a form using only **I-FETCH** and **I-STORE**, plus literal constants as necessary. Figure 4-9 shows **TUPLE-FETCH.2** rewritten as an **I-FETCH** and a literal offset. In both this case and in the previous example, triggers for the literal instructions were derived from inputs to the original program graph instruction.

Array creation instructions are expanded in a manner similar to that for the TTDA. Specifically, one dimensional array creation instances are expanded into **MAKE-I-STRUCTURE** instructions, while higher dimensioned array creations are expanded into calls to library routines.

DEF. All **DEF** encapsulators (outermost encapsulator of any procedure codeblock) are rewritten to parameterized **FASTCALL-DEF**s. **DEF** abstracts both the mechanism of passing arguments between contexts and the mechanism of conditionally unpacking argument chains sent from

---

[34]For the **MAKE-I-VECTOR** instructions, the possibilities are *"tuple"* and *"string"*.

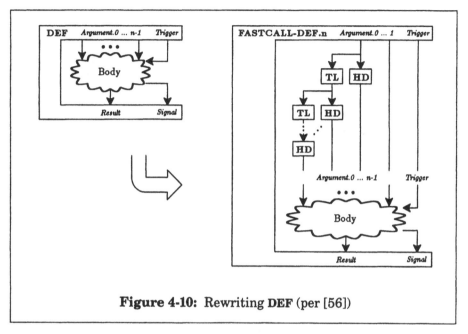

Figure 4-10: Rewriting DEF (per [56])

APPLYs. Rewriting separates these two abstractions. The argument chain unpacking is explicitly represented by a set of **HD** and **TL** instructions which take apart the list of arguments. Conditional execution of these unpacking instructions is a consequence of the method of triggering SQ's. The gist of the method relies on

- Suspension of the ARGUMENT CHAIN continuation, which contains the first **HD** and **TL** instructions. Both of these require the argument chain. If no chain is sent, as in the **DIRECT-APPLY** case, these instructions will not execute.

- Initiation of continuations for the remainder of the unpacking as part of the argument chain continuation.

Figure 4-10 shows the complete transformation. The **FASTCALL-DEF** is parameterized with the number of non-trigger arguments (n) of the original **DEF** encapsulator.

APPLY, DIRECT-APPLY, and APPLY-UNSATISFIED. APPLY instructions are rewritten into **IF** encapsulators which test the closure arguments for readiness, *i.e.*, that all arguments are present, and conditionally invoke the procedure via **FASTCALL-APPLY** if ready (Figure 4-11). If the closure

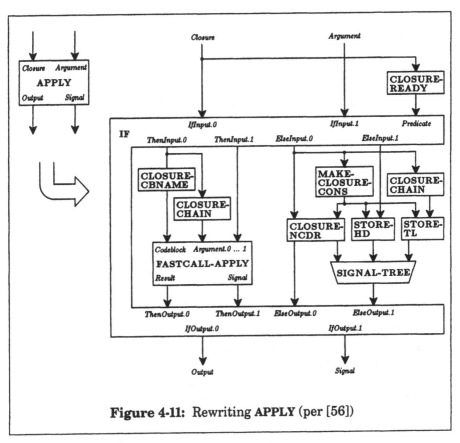

Figure 4-11: Rewriting APPLY (per [56])

is not yet ready (*i.e.*, there are still missing arguments), the existing argument chain is extended by one CONS cell, the head of which contains the argument and the tail of which contains a pointer to the old argument chain. A new closure containing a pointer to the new chain is created, and the counter of arguments remaining is decremented.

DIRECT-APPLY is rewritten, essentially, into the TRUE-branch of an APPLY save that all arguments are connected to the FASTCALL-APPLY rather than just one. APPLY-UNSATISFIED is rewritten into the false branch of an APPLY.

FASTCALL-APPLY. All instances of FASTCALL-APPLY, including those created by rewriting APPLY and DIRECT-APPLY, are rewritten into a form which exposes the embedded dynamic arcs. Essentially, this is consistent

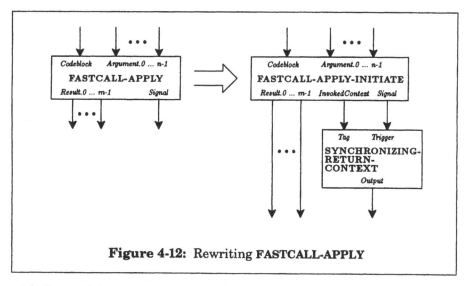

Figure 4-12: Rewriting **FASTCALL-APPLY**

with the split transaction nature of **I-FETCH**: one instruction initiates the fetch while others synchronize prior to using the result. In the case of **FASTCALL-APPLY**, one instruction initiates the invocation, and a second instruction (**SYNCHRONIZING-RETURN-CONTEXT**) synchronizes on the return signal and then deallocates the invocation's resources. The translation is depicted in Figure 4-12.

Partitioning Constraints

Earlier, the issues of safe partitioning were illustrated. In this section, the notion of safely partitioning a dataflow graph is more completely developed. It is again assumed that the input graphs are well-formed and well-connected. Since there is the potential of introducing deadlock as a result of partitioning a dataflow graph, the major goal of this section is to develop a set of partitioning constraints which will demonstrably avoid the introduction of deadlock.

Partitioning a graph into SQ's, wherein the instructions are totally ordered, may imply the addition of arcs into the graph to effect sequentialization. First, the issues of introducing additional arcs into an otherwise acyclic graph are identified. Next, the Method of Dependence Sets, a simple yet safe algorithm for partitioning dataflow graphs, is presented. Finally, the behavior of the algorithm is analyzed. It is shown that, despite the introduction of arcs, deadlock-inducing cycles are not created.

Adding Arcs. In order to guarantee liveness of the partitioned graph, it is essential no cycle be introduced into the partitioned graph which cannot be resolved. Recall that the partitioned graph contains only SQ nodes, each representing some nonempty subset of the nodes in the unpartitioned graph. Moreover, the instructions in each such subset are totally ordered. This sequentialization can interact with existing dependences in the graph, leading to a static cycle. Depending upon the interpretation model for sequentialized SQ's, deadlock may result.

> **Definition 4-1:** An UNRESOLVABLE STATIC CYCLE is a directed cycle of SQ's in a partitioned dataflow graph for which no schedule of SQ executions can terminate.

Given that instructions within an SQ are to be interpreted sequentially, it is clear that arbitrary partitioning of an acyclic graph into SQ's can result in unresolvable static cycles, a sufficient condition for deadlock. This is reasonably obvious — the partial order represented by a dataflow graph captures all and only the necessary inter-instruction dependences. Imposing further constraints, *viz.*, sequential execution, on a graph is tantamount to adding additional dependence arcs. Doing so in a haphazard fashion can clearly introduce a cycle where there was none.

An example of how partitioning can give rise to a static cycle was shown in Figure 4-2. In order to avoid deadlock, it is necessary either to prohibit such cycles or to devise methods for resolving them. Sarkar and Hennessy [51] choose the former tack and impose a convexity constraint on the partitioning — static cycles can therefore never arise. As an alternative to their technique, it is possible to use an SQ interpretation model which allows such cycles to be resolved. One can imagine a partitioning in which the ability to resolve a cycle only means that the order of instructions in an SQ must follow the topological ordering of the dataflow graph, and that there must be a notion of SQ suspension and resumption based on the absence and presence, respectively, of data on inter-SQ arcs. One possible mechanism which allows this behavior and which is efficient was addressed in Section 3.3.

Unfortunately, in order to avoid partitioning-induced deadlock, it is not sufficient simply to resolve all static cycles. I-Structure storage has introduced the notion of dynamic arcs between producer and consumer. Since these arcs are input-dependent, they are not explicitly expressed in the graph and are therefore not amenable to static analysis. They impose no less of a constraint, however. Consider an unpartitioned graph, augmented with all potential arcs from producers to consumers through I-Structure slots. This graph would form the basis for a kind of static analysis; partitioning would be constrained by the ability to resolve any cycles so introduced.

> **Definition 4-2:** An UNRESOLVABLE DYNAMIC CYCLE is a directed cycle of SQ's in a partitioned dataflow graph, augmented with the input-specific dynamic arcs, for which no schedule of SQ executions can terminate.

The algorithm presented in the next section allows the partitioning of dataflow graphs without the introduction of either static or dynamic cycles.

The Method of Dependence Sets. The Method of Dependence Sets (MDS) is a simple algorithm for safely partitioning dataflow graphs. It seeks to avoid the problems of static and dynamic cycles by uniquely naming each FETCH-like output, and then grouping together all and only those instructions which depend directly or indirectly upon the same set of names. The following definitions are in order:

> **Definition 4-3:** The INPUT DEPENDENCE SET for instruction i (written $IDS(i)$) in a well-connected graph is the union of the output dependence sets of all instructions from which it receives input. The input dependence set of the root instruction is $\emptyset$. The input dependence set for instructions with no inputs is likewise defined as $\emptyset$.

> **Definition 4-4:** The OUTPUT DEPENDENCE SET for a given output o of a given instruction i (written $ODS(i,o)$) is either the instruction's input dependence set if the output is not FETCH-like, or the union of the instruction's input dependence set with a singleton set made up of an identifier which uniquely names the given output if it is.

Note that it is a FETCH-like instruction's output, and not the instruction itself, with which is associated a change of dependence set. One may view the output-associated identifiers as unique colors.

Now, assume a well-connected dataflow graph $G=(V,E,R)$, where

- V is the set of graph instructions.

- E: $\{(i,j) \mid i,j \in V$ and j depends directly on $i\}$ (the set of static dependence arcs)

- $R \in V$ and R is the root instruction.

Algorithm 4-5:
METHOD OF DEPENDENCE SETS(G)
For each output o of R, compute ODS(R,o). Traverse graph G from R per topological ordering[35], selecting an instruction $i \in V$ to expand. For each such instruction,

- *Calculate IDS(i).*

- *Assign the generated machine instructions, in order, to an SQ corresponding to IDS(i). SQ's are selected such that for any two graph instructions $i,j \in V$*

    IDS(i)=IDS(j)⇔SQ(i)=SQ(j)

  The SQ denoted by IDS(R)=∅ is called the DISTINGUISHED SQ.

- *For each output o of instruction i, calculate ODS(i,o).*

Table 4-1: Resulting Partition	
Instruction	Dependence set
I-STORE(0)	∅
I-FETCH(i)	∅
I-FETCH(j)	∅
I-FETCH(1)	∅
I-FETCH(2)	∅
+1	$\{\alpha\}$
I-STORE(1)	$\{\alpha\}$
-2	$\{\beta\}$
I-STORE(2)	$\{\beta\}$
.	$\{\gamma\}$

Per the characterization of dynamic arcs in the last Chapter, FETCH-like

---

[35]Such an ordering is specified in Algorithm 4-11, p. 131.

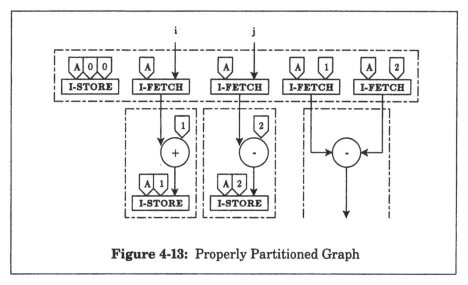

Figure 4-13: Properly Partitioned Graph

outputs represent long-latency operations. Viewed another way, it is the virtual gate (*c.f.*, Figure 3-1) which must be pushed to the boundary of the unit of schedulability. This is done by forcing all sink instructions fed by the gate into a new SQ. These sink instructions execute only when the **I-FETCH** and **I-STORE** upon which they depend have completed.

Applying the definitions to the graph in Figure 4-3 and using α, β, and γ for unique names results in the assignments of input dependence sets to instructions as shown in the Table (assume that vector A and the indices i,j are derived from the root with dependence set $\varnothing$).

Since each distinct combination of dynamic arcs denotes a single SQ, dynamic scheduling can change to match the dynamic dependences. The correctly partitioned graph is shown in Figure 4-13. The determination of synchronization points is also straightforward: each dependence (arc) which crosses SQ boundaries must be explicitly synchronized by the consumer, or sink, SQ. Consumers in the same SQ as the instruction producing a value need not perform synchronization. It is implicit in the static scheduling of instructions within the SQ (these are exactly the static synchronized and static unsynchronized arcs of Section 3.2).

Properties of MDS. MDS collects together into SQ's all and only those instructions with identical dynamic dependence requirements. That is, every instruction in an SQ depends directly or indirectly on the same set of FETCH-like outputs and I-STOREs. Each resulting SQ is a set of subgraphs. Disjoint subgraphs in an SQ have neither a static dependence nor a dynamic dependence between them. The former is obvious — otherwise, they would not be disjoint. The latter is less obvious, but follows immediately from the definitions. A dynamic dependence would imply FETCH-like instruction outputs feeding sink instructions, which would necessarily have forced the sink instructions to appear in a different SQ.

This simple assertion has a powerful effect on the manner in which SQ instructions can be sequentialized. For an SQ which contains but a single subgraph, the ordering must adhere to the subgraph's topological constraints. For an SQ with more than one subgraph, the instructions from any one subgraph must be topologically ordered, but there is no cross-subgraph constraint. Consequently, in an SQ containing subgraphs A and B, instructions from B may follow all the instructions of A, or conversely. Alternatively, instructions from A and B may be interleaved. The point is that, because there cannot be a dynamic dependence between them, introduction of sequentializing arcs cannot interfere with essential dynamic instruction ordering.

Can cycles, either static or dynamic, ever arise among the SQ's partitioned by MDS? The following two theorems address this question directly.

Theorem 4-6: Partitioning an acyclic dataflow graph by MDS results in a graph which is free of static cycles.

In order to prove this, it is necessary first to establish a few other facts, specifically, (1) that where there is a dependence between two SQ'S, there is a proper subset relationship between their dependence sets and (2) that transitivity of this relation holds.

Lemma 4-7: Inter-Instruction Dependence: For all instructions $i,j \in V$, if $(i,j) \in E$ then $IDS(j) \supseteq IDS(i)$.

Proof: Follows directly from Definition 4-3.

□

Lemma 4-8: Cross-SQ Dependence: For all instructions $i,j \in V$, if $(i,j) \in E$ and $SQ(i) \neq SQ(j)$ then $IDS(j) \supset IDS(i)$.

Proof: (by contradiction)

From Lemma 4-7, $IDS(j) \supseteq IDS(i)$. Assume that $IDS(j)=IDS(i)$. But from Algorithm 4-5, it then follows that $SQ(j)=SQ(i)$.

☐

Lemma 4-9: Dependence Transitivity: For all instructions $i,j,k,l \in V$, if $(i,j) \in E$, $(k,l) \in E$, $SQ(j)=SQ(k)$, and $SQ(i) \neq SQ(j) \neq SQ(l)$, then $IDS(l) \supset IDS(i)$.

Proof:

$IDS(j) \supset IDS(i)$	[1] Lemma 4-8
$IDS(l) \supset IDS(k)$	[2] Lemma 4-8
$IDS(j)=IDS(k)$	[3] Algorithm 4-5
$IDS(l) \supset IDS(j)$	[4] by 2 and 3
$IDS(l) \supset IDS(i)$	[5] transitivity — 4,1

☐

The theorem can now be proved rather simply.

Proof: (by contradiction)

Consider a cycle of dependence arcs among a set of distinct SQ'S $A,B,....$ Then, by Lemma 4-9 it follows immediately that $IDS(A) \supset IDS(A)$.

☐

Theorem 4-10: Partitioning an acyclic dataflow graph by MDS results in a graph which is free of dynamic cycles.

Theorem 4-6 states that the result of partitioning of an acyclic graph by MDS is itself acyclic. Augmenting this graph with all possible input-specific dynamic arcs raises the possibility of cycles containing one or more dynamic arcs. It follows from the definitions that a dynamic cycle cannot occur within a single SQ (as discussed above). It remains to show that no cross-SQ cycles exist.

> **Proof:** (by contradiction)
>
> Assume a cycle among two or more SQ's wherein one or more of the cycle-forming arcs is dynamic. Because a dynamic arc is involved, there must be an **I-STORE** instruction i in the cycle. Consider this **I-STORE** instruction and the SQ in which it resides. By the assumption and Algorithm 4-5, this SQ must depend on the dynamic arc. But, again by Algorithm 4-5, all instructions in the SQ, including i, depend on the dynamic arc. This is true independent of any sequentializing arcs which may or may not be added to the SQ. Here is a situation of a dependence which violates I-structure semantics. Hence, either there is an error in the original program, or the assumed cycle cannot exist.

□

Summary. In this section, a partitioning algorithm has been introduced which groups together all and only those instructions with identical dynamic arc dependences. It has been shown that the extra arcs introduced by the algorithm do not interfere with essential instruction orderings, that static cycles are not created, and that dynamic cycles are not possible.

Operand Storage Allocation

This section examines the mapping of arcs in the graph into proper dynamic storage. Such storage is invocation specific and, by analogy with von Neumann machines, a frame, or array of directly indexed slots is the model.

The problems of allocating invocation-specific operand storage can be divided into two categories: those which can be reduced to analogous ones in a von Neumann environment and those which are unique to parallel processing. For the sake of completeness, both are presented here. The latter category has received considerably more attention in this study, however. To that end, a number of known storage conservation techniques which apply to the former category were simply not implemented in the prototype compiler. It was therefore deemed sufficient to allocate one slot in the frame for each instruction output in the graph[36] with the following exceptions:

- **Merged arcs**, *e.g.*, the outputs of the *Then* and *Else* blocks of an **IF** encapsulator, cause instruction outputs to be mapped to the same frame slot.

- **Loop variables** are mapped statically to frame slots, but the slots are re-used in a carefully controlled fashion across iterations. This important optimization is described below.

The Frame. Codeblocks are classified as PROCEDURE CODEBLOCKS or INNER LOOP CODEBLOCKS as described in Section 1.1. Their frames differ in the way arguments and constants are handled. The remainder of the frame structure is identical.

Slots are reserved in both kinds of frames as follows: the first slot contains a frame descriptor which points to the return area in the caller's own frame. This frame descriptor, therefore, must denote a globally unique frame address. The second slot contains the argument chain I-structure descriptor unless any of the following is true, in which case the slot will be empty:

- It is an inner loop codeblock, in which case arguments are sent directly and no chain is used.

---

[36]Frame slots are assumed to be inaccessible outside of the given execution context. Moreover, the values held in frame slots have a lifetime which is always less than or equal to the lifetime of the frame and generally much less. It is possible and highly desirable to fold the compiled codeblock such that slots can be re-used. This problem is equivalent to register assignment for traditional architectures with the added constraint of multiple continuations per codeblock. This introduces nondeterminism into the matter of deciding when a slot will no longer be referenced; in the case that the producer of a value and all of its consumers are not within the same SQ, dynamic methods (or loosely bounded static methods) are necessary. In that the compilation scheme proposed here does not partition a codeblock into SQ's until after frame slot assignment, such folding is not possible.

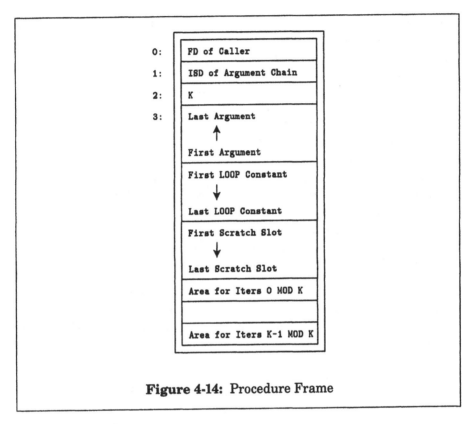

Figure 4-14: Procedure Frame

- It is a procedure codeblock but the arity is zero or one, in which case a chain is unnecessary.

- It is a procedure codeblock but is being invoked by **DIRECT-APPLY**, in which case the arguments are sent directly as in the inner loop case.

The third slot is reserved for the invocation-time value of K, the bound on the degree of loop unfolding. The major difference between procedure and inner loop codeblocks shows up in the argument/constant area.

Procedure Codeblocks (Figure 4-14): A procedure codeblock may or may not include an outer **LOOP**, but in any event, it includes at most one. This **LOOP** may require a constant area to hold loop invariant values. Such constants are computed after procedure invocation but prior to execution of the loop. Therefore, constants are distinct from procedure arguments and are stored separately in the frame. Loop constants are as-

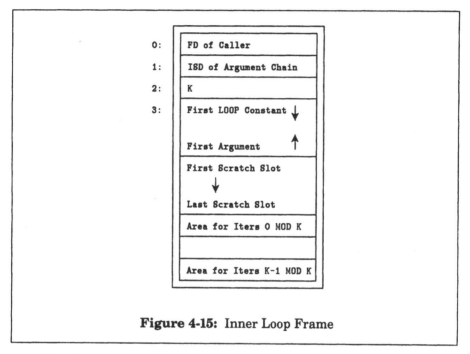

0:	FD of Caller
1:	ISD of Argument Chain
2:	K
3:	First LOOP Constant ↓
	First Argument ↑
	First Scratch Slot
	↓
	Last Scratch Slot
	Area for Iters 0 MOD K
	Area for Iters K-1 MOD K

Figure 4-15: Inner Loop Frame

signed ordinal indices in the graph, and these indices are mapped to off-sets in the constant area of the frame. Arguments are handled by mapping the last to a fixed offset (3) in the frame, with the second-to-last occupying offset 4, and so on. Arguments are thus mapped in reverse order, from last to first, in the frame. The reason for this is slightly subtle.

The procedure linkage constraints imposed by the closure-based application scheme dictate that the **APPLY** instruction which detects that the arity is satisfied will forward the last argument (as supplied to the **APPLY**) and the argument chain descriptor (part of the closure) to the invoked procedure. Since the arity of the called procedure is not known, in general, at the time the caller is compiled, the means of sending the last argument must be independent of arity. Hence, it is the last argument, rather than the first, which appears at a fixed address in the frame. Note that this limitation does not affect the implementation of **DIRECT-APPLY** since it is specifically in this case that the called procedure's arity is known.

Inner Loop Codeblocks (Figure 4-15): An inner loop codeblock always includes a **LOOP** encapsulator. The loop constants are handled differently

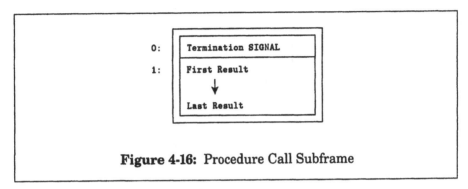

Figure 4-16: Procedure Call Subframe

than in the case of a procedure codeblock. Here, the arguments to the codeblock include the loop constants. Therefore, there is no explicit constant area separate from the argument area, and the overhead of storing constants is subsumed by the passing of arguments to the codeblock.

Following the arguments and constants, slots are used as necessary to store arc values for the remainder of the codeblock. This area is largely unstructured, and slots are individually allocated. The exception to this rule is the case of codeblock invocation. Since procedure codeblocks in general return a result and a signal, and inner loop codeblocks return multiple results and a signal, a decision must be made. The caller can send multiple slot pointers to the called codeblock, one for each thing to be returned, or the caller can reserve a contiguous block of slots and send only a single pointer with the understanding of how multiple pointers should be derived from it. The latter scheme is by far more economical in terms of network traffic. Such contiguous blocks of slots are PROCEDURE CALL SUBFRAMES, and their format is depicted in Figure 4-16.

Up to this point, all slots have been allocated statically. Further, the use of such slots will always adhere to the write-once, read-many discipline. Not surprisingly, loops confuse this order. From experience with the TTDA [10], the benefits of exploiting dynamic loop unfolding and inter-iteration parallelism are clear [19]. The degree to which a loop can unfold (the number of concurrent iterations plus 1: K) is an invocation-time parameter. Iteration specific resources are re-used *modulo K*. In the domain of dataflow machines, the complexities of the necessary dynamic naming and dynamic storage management are masked by the implicit tag manipulation rules and the waiting-matching hardware. In the hybrid, names and slots are allocated and deallocated at invocation boundaries;

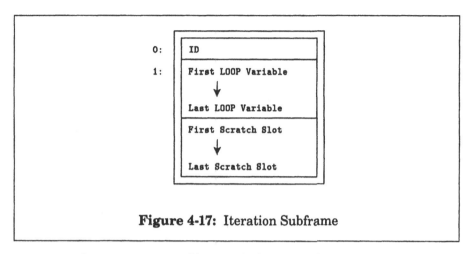

Figure 4-17: Iteration Subframe

consequently, management of loop unfolding introduces a dynamic character to slot allocation.

The hybrid framework can indeed support the dynamic unfolding of loops and inter-iteration parallelism. Each instance of an iteration requires access to the program text, access to loop constants, and its own private working area in the frame. The latter is provided through the use of the continuation-specific index registers through which indirect access to iteration specific state is possible. Within the Predicate and Body of the LOOP, slot numbers are assigned in a virtual frame, called an ITERATION SUBFRAME (Figure 4-17). The 0th slot in each subframe is reserved for an Iteration Descriptor. The next n slots hold the n loop variables, with the remainder of the frame for loop temporaries. It is assumed that these subframes will be recycled *modulo K*, and the assumptions about write-once slots break down.

Upon invocation of a LOOP-containing codeblock, the amount of frame space allocated will be $x+Ky$ slots to accommodate both the x non-LOOP slots as well as K instances of the y slots necessary for the unfolded LOOP.

Assignment, Propagation, and Constraints. After rewriting, the only remaining encapsulators are IF, FASTCALL-DEF, and LOOP. Encapsulators have outputs on both the exterior surface and on surfaces which enclose the basic blocks. Certain of these outputs are NONTRANSPARENT, *i.e.*, in the final expansion of the encapsulator, instructions will be

Table 4-2: Frame Slot Mappings		
Instruction or Encapsulator	Port Name	Slot Mapping
LITERAL	Output	*none* if immediate *assigned - shared* otherwise
LOOP-CONSTANT	Output	*assigned - loop constant area*
I-FETCH	Output	*assigned - argument area* if arg *assigned - otherwise*
IF	IfOutput ThenInput ElseInput ThenOutput ElseOutput IfInput	*assigned* *propagated - IfInput* *propagated - IfInput* *constrained - IfOutput* *constrained - IfOutput* *none*
LOOP	LoopOutput PredicateInput BodyInput BodyOutput LoopInput PredicateOutput	*assigned* *assigned* *propagated - PredicateOutput* *constrained - loop variable area* *constrained - loop variable area* *none*
FASTCALL-DEF	Argument Trigger	*assigned - argument area* *assigned - frame descriptor*
FASTCALL-APPLY-INITIATE	Signal Result	*assigned - termination signal* *assigned - result area*
OTHERS	Output	*assigned*

generated which themselves produce the value associated with the output. Other outputs are TRANSPARENT — the value associated with the output will have been created by an instruction other than the encapsulator itself and will appear elsewhere as an input to the encapsulator. It is possible to statically classify every output of every encapsulator as transparent or nontransparent, and for transparent outputs to identify the input or inputs from which the value will come.

Frame slots must be ASSIGNed to nontransparent outputs and PROPAGATEd to transparent ones. Assignment implies that an output is marked as the originator of a value or set of values which will occupy a specified frame slot. In the event that arcs are merged (as in the LOOP and **IF** encapsulators), there will be two distinct instructions whose output arcs are mapped to the same slot number. This presents no problem of semantics for the same reason that **MERGE**s in the TTDA present no problem — the one-in, one-out property is always preserved when the schema (encapsulator) is viewed as a whole. In this case, the mapping to slot numbers is called CONSTRAINed. The table shows, for each type of instruction port, the kind of frame slot mapping which applies.

Method. The method of mapping arcs to frame slot numbers in a codeblock is to traverse the graph from the root, which is always a single **FASTCALL-DEF**, first assigning nontransparent frame slot numbers to the root's outputs, then mapping body arcs to frame slots. The former process is straightforward; for each argument output of the **FASTCALL-DEF** to which is connected a sink instruction, assign the corresponding predefined frame slot number. If this **FASTCALL-DEF** was the result of having rewritten a **DEF**, there will be two argument outputs, the argument chain (slot 1) and the last argument (slot 3). Otherwise, there will be n arguments, assigned to slots beginning with slot 3. If the trigger output has a sink instruction, it is assigned slot 0 (the return frame descriptor).

The latter process of mapping arcs in a basic block to frame slots is slightly more complex. First, for each instruction in the basic block, non-transparent frame slot numbers are assigned. Then, for each encapsulator, transparent frame slot numbers are propagated, constraints are applied, and mappings of arcs within the encapsulator's basic blocks are done recursively.

In the case of literals, several optimizations are performed. First, because certain literals are representable as immediate values, no frame slots need be assigned. A majority of literals are covered by this case, *e.g.*, small integers used to index CONSes and tuples. Second, it is unnecessary to reserve more than one frame slot for the same non-immediate literal value; instead, an association list is built during frame slot assignment to record the hardware type and value of each non-immediate literal and its assigned frame slot. Multiple literal instructions calling out the same value will use the same frame slot. Such frame slots are initialized during the prelude of the codeblock, and references to these slots need never cause suspension.

LOOPs present a special problem in addition to the issue of merged arcs discussed above. Since slots associated with circulating loop variables will be re-written from iteration to iteration, it must be the case that

- no rewriting of a slot is visible outside the **LOOP** (as would be the case of instruction A feeding instruction B as well as a **LOOP** input). A similar problem exists for non-immediate literals used as inputs.

- immediate literals used to initialize circulating variables are copied to frame slots prior to **LOOP** entry (an immediate can't be re-written).

- no body input slot may be rewritten until the existing value is no longer needed in the current iteration.

- **LOOP** outputs are not accessible until the **LOOP** terminates. Using frame slots as the sole means of synchronization could potentially lead to the interpretation of an intermediate result as the final **LOOP** output.

Non-**LOOP** codeblocks are acyclic and, as a result, each arc will denote at most one value for each invocation. Consequently, the corresponding frame slots are written at most once per invocation. **LOOP**s present the possibility of re-writing slots during an invocation. As discussed previously, mapping of arcs within a **LOOP** is handled specially. While all other codeblock arcs are mapped into a single frame namespace, **LOOP** arcs are mapped to a separate namespace. When a codeblock is invoked, space is allocated to hold a single copy of the non-**LOOP** slots, and additional space is allocated to hold K copies of the **LOOP** slots with the intent of allowing $K-1$ consecutive iteration bodies to run concurrently.

Keeping changes local to the **LOOP** is easily handled by simple analysis of each **LOOP** input — if it is not the sole sink, an **IDENTITY** instruction is inserted between the source and the **LOOP** input[37].

---

[37]Note that it is not enough that the **LOOP** encapsulator is the only sink for each source — it is possible that a single source feeds two distinct **LOOP** inputs. Unless these are explicitly separated by an **IDENTITY** instruction, the two **LOOP** variables will be aliases.

Summary. This section has reviewed the problem of allocating dynamic storage for an invocation as an extension to von Neumann methods. It has been shown that in order to exploit parallelism, *e.g.*, across iterations, it is necessary to allocate significantly more storage than would be necessary in a sequential von Neumann paradigm. Another manifestation, although not explored here, is the difficulty (and additional storage space) of folding the graph to permit re-use of slots during execution in the manner of traditional register allocation techniques. The difficulty, again, arises out of the multi-threaded (parallel) nature of the model.

Machine Code Generation and Partitioning

After the graph is re-written into a simpler form and frame slots have been assigned, machine code can be generated. This process is done by simultaneously translating graph instructions into machine instructions and partitioning the generated instructions into SQ's. Both activities involve correctly reflecting the data dependences in the final codeblock module. As shall become clear, the process is distinctly different than that of the TTDA. Static dependences constrain code order within SQ's; dynamic dependences constrain the partitioning of code into SQ's and the choice of synchronization points.

Representation of Scheduling Quanta. As the graph is translated, it is partitioned according to the constraints in Section 4.3. The internal representation of a scheduling quantum is shown in Figure 4-18. This abstraction is responsible for being the repository of translated instructions in the SQ. More importantly, this abstraction is used to enforce the constraints imposed by the architecture regarding register usage (fixed number, values not preserved across suspensions). The abstraction also summarizes the inputs to the SQ (these will always be frame slots — immediate literals are uninteresting, and registers can never be SQ inputs) and the termination signal slots.

Within the compiler, virtually all register references are symbolic. Allocation and deallocation of register numbers is automatic. The mapping of register names to register numbers is handled by the SQ abstraction, and invalidation of names across potentially suspensive instructions is enforced.

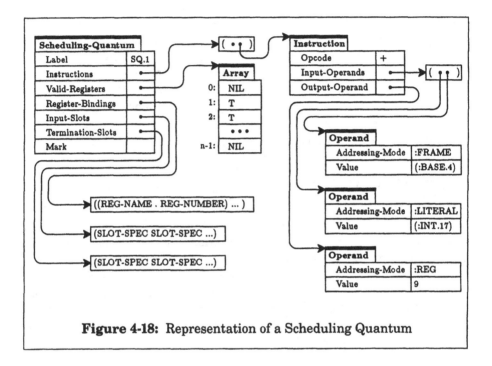

Figure 4-18: Representation of a Scheduling Quantum

Mechanism for Translating a Graph Instruction. Translation proceeds in a straightforward manner. The algorithm is divided into a DRIVER, which understands graph structure but nothing of the semantics of the instructions to be translated, and a set of EXPANDERS, one for each graph instruction. Expanders know nothing of graph structure and simply specify the translation of a graph instruction to machine code as a function of the graph instruction's properties, *e.g.*, number of inputs and outputs, instruction parameters, and opcode. The specification of an expander is mechanically transformed into a function which performs the translation and then recursively calls the driver on the instruction's outputs. The driver selects graph instructions for expansion when and only when all of the instruction's inputs have been expanded. This simple technique produces code within SQ's which is sequentialized according to the topological ordering of the original program graph.

The driver is expressed as a few very simple functions which traverse the graph. The *Expand* function invokes the appropriate expander for each graph instruction; the expander in turn invokes *ExpandOutputs* as appropriate. This process treats encapsulators as instructions.

Algorithm 4-11:
GENERATE(Graph)

- *For each Instruction in Graph, mark it with an EnablingCount equal to the number of arcs incident on its Exterior surface.*

- *Invoke EXPAND on the Root Instruction.*

Algorithm 4-12: *EXPAND(Instruction)*
Unless Instruction is marked,

- *Mark it*

- *Invoke its Expander*

Algorithm 4-13: *EXPANDOUTPUTS(Instruction)*

- *For each Output on all surfaces of Instruction, Invoke EXPANDSINK on Instruction and Output*

- *If Instruction is an encapsulator, note the subordinate SQ descriptors created in expanding the instructions connected to the non-exterior outputs.*

Algorithm 4-14: *EXPANDSINK(SourceInstruction,SourceOutput)*
For each SinkInstruction connected to SourceOutput of SourceInstruction,
When the arc to SinkInstruction is incident on its Exterior surface,

- *Decrement its EnablingCount.*

- *When the resulting EnablingCount is zero, mark the arc and invoke EXPAND on SinkInstruction.*

The astute reader will recognize these algorithms as a kind of static dataflow interpreter. This should not be surprising in that the hybrid philosophy seeks to translate static scheduling constraints of a dataflow graph into a set of partially ordered sequential instruction threads.

The following operations are common to the expansion of each type of graph instruction. They are added automatically to the specification of the semantics of each graph instruction, thereby hiding details of the representation of SQ's and the vagaries of the synchronization mechanisms of the model.

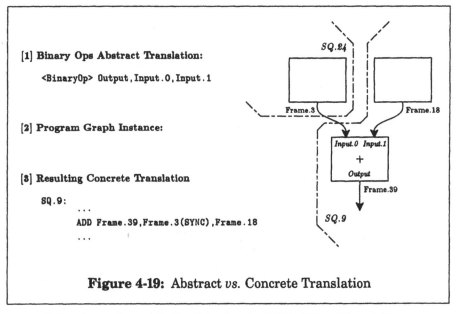

[1] **Binary Ops Abstract Translation:**

    `<BinaryOp> Output,Input.0,Input.1`

[2] **Program Graph Instance:**

[3] **Resulting Concrete Translation**

    `SQ.9:`

        `...`

        `ADD Frame.39,Frame.3(SYNC),Frame.18`

        `...`

Figure 4-19: Abstract *vs.* Concrete Translation

- **Selection of an SQ**: Partitioning by MDS (Algorithm 4-5) requires, for each graph instruction, the computation of its input dependence set which uniquely defines the SQ to which the expanded instructions belong. At compile time, an association is maintained between dependence sets and SQ's. New quanta are allocated each time a computed dependence set fails to map to an existing quantum. SQ's are static objects which must be explicitly triggered at runtime; therefore, the creation of a new quantum implies the need to install a trigger in an existing SQ.

- **Computation of addressing modes**: In translating a DFPG instruction, reference is made to the input operands in the abstract — each input is an arc which logically denotes a value held in some physical resource, *e.g.*, in the frame, in a register, or in the instruction itself as in the case of an immediate literal. Each arc and the instruction which feeds it uniquely define the hardware resource represented. The operand addressing information can therefore be computed by simple analysis of the instructions which feed the one in question. See Figure 4-19.

The compiler records a history of registers as output operands. Because the driver traverses the graph according to topological ordering, it is possible to flag invalid references to registers at compile time.

- **Addition of Synchronization**: By MDS, it is known where synchronization will be required — for any input to any graph instruction, synchronization is necessary at operand fetch time if the input comes from another SQ, directly (a static arc) or indirectly (a dynamic arc). The compile-time representation of SQ's makes this determination straightforward.

- **Test for Suspensiveness**: Once synchronization tests have been applied, it is known (again, at compile time) if an instruction cannot suspend. When an instruction can be proved non-suspensive, no updating of the register allocation information in its SQ is necessary. If, however, this cannot be proved, the instruction's SQ abstraction is updated to show that no subsequent instruction may make reference to a value previously stored in any register.

Machine Code Generation. The next task is the (nearly) context-free expansion of graph instructions into machine instructions, with no concern for the issues of partitioning, operand addressing, register allocation, synchronization, and so on as discussed above. The expansion is, however, a function of opcode, number of inputs and outputs, and other local, instance specific information.

Signals and triggers were introduced into DFPG's to make them well-connected, *i.e.*, to guarantee that each instruction which should fire does fire (triggering), and that it is possible to determine when every instruction in a block which should fire has fired (signalling). Triggering and signalling are implicit under the von Neumann instruction execution model because there is only one locus of control. In a dataflow machine, however, it is much less straightforward. Certain instructions which themselves require no input, *e.g.*, constant generators, must be explicitly initiated, hence the need for triggers. Other instructions which produce no output but are only executed for effect, *e.g.*, **I-STORE**, must be explicitly tested for completion, hence the need for signals.

How do signals and triggers apply to the hybrid instruction execution model? Not surprisingly, the von Neumann style of implicit signalling and triggering applies within an SQ, but the dataflow model of explicit signals and triggers must be enforced between SQ's. It would not do, for instance, to construct an SQ which receives only constant inputs and not to provide a means to initiate this SQ. Similarly, it would be necessary to provide some mechanism to detect termination of an SQ which produces no arc-carried results.

A simple technique is to represent signal and trigger arcs explicitly in the compiled hybrid program. This, of course, is unnecessary and misses the opportunity for some good optimizations. Assume that the graph is well connected. In what situations are signals and triggers essential?

Triggers: Literal constant instructions are the prime motivator for triggers. But as described previously, constants are handled by first eliminating all those which can be represented as immediate values, and second by loading frame slots during the codeblock's prelude with all other literals. Moreover, MDS will never create an SQ which has only literal inputs. This follows by definition — an SQ depends directly on some set of dynamic arcs. It can be argued, therefore, that explicit representation of trigger arcs across SQ boundaries because of the need to trigger literal constants is unnecessary.

Note, however, that the mechanism of synchronization relies on an eager reading of a frame slot, possibly resulting in suspension of the SQ which attempted the read. Hence, it is necessary to initiate, or trigger, every SQ which will ultimately be expected to compute. This does not mean that all SQ's within a codeblock should be triggered at codeblock initiation. Rather, it means that SQ's should be triggered when and only when the graph implies a triggering of any instruction in the SQ.

Such triggering is most conveniently done when a new SQ is formed by virtue of a dynamic arc. That is, the compilation of an instruction such as **I-FETCH** will include both the code to perform the fetch and the (implicit) code to trigger the SQ which was generated to receive the result[38,39].

Signals: Signals are synthetic outputs generated by instructions which would otherwise have none, *e.g.*, **I-STORE**. In the dataflow paradigm where each instruction is its own scheduling quantum, the primary evidence of an instruction having fired and, hence, the proof that a

---

[38]The exception to this rule occurs in the SQ which reads the argument chain slot. There, the trigger is installed in the distinguished SQ. This allows the codeblock to be properly triggered irrespective of the way it was invoked (**APPLY** or **DIRECT-APPLY**).

[39]A pathological case arises, using this method, whereby SQ's may be created which are completely empty or which contain nothing other than triggers for other SQ's. This case is handled by the SQ structural optimizer, discussed in a later section.

codeblock has terminated is the production of an output value. Signals are therefore necessary for proving that instructions like **I-STORE** have fired. Signals are collected by **SIGNAL-TREE** instructions, and summary signal information is preserved and propagated from the innermost levels of a codeblock all the way to the signal input of the **FASTCALL-DEF**.

In the hybrid paradigm, signal generating instructions may be compiled within scheduling quanta along with other instructions. For that reason, adding signal outputs to **I-STORE** instructions in order to detect firing is not strictly necessary. The requirement is more appropriately to be able to detect SQ termination and to be able to deduce firing. Moreover, explicit representation of signal arcs as synchronizable frame slots is only necessary between SQ's. Intra-SQ signalling can be implicit in instruction order.

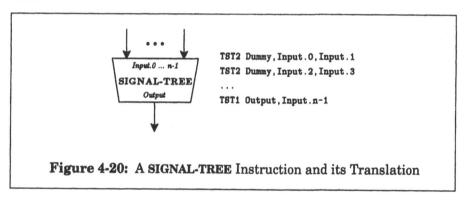

Figure 4-20: A **SIGNAL-TREE** Instruction and its Translation

SIGNAL-TREE instructions, therefore, need not be compiled as a tree of instructions which serve to test each individual signal (Figure 4-20). It is sufficient to generate code which merely tests for termination of all the SQ's whose instructions are connected to the **SIGNAL-TREE**. This can be done by arranging the storing of a value into some frame slot as the last activity of an SQ and then testing that slot. In many cases, this is an easily satisfied constraint on code order in the SQ which requires no additional instructions and no additional slots. In the rare case that this is not possible, *e.g.*, in an SQ which must end with an instruction which does not unconditionally write to a known slot, an extra instruction and slot can be used as a dummy signal. In any case, there is no need to test signals which originate in the same SQ as the **SIGNAL-TREE** itself. The compiled signal tree tests each such slot in turn, suspending execution until the signal is written.

If codeblock termination detection were the only need for signals (it is not), signal arcs and SIGNAL-TREEs could be eliminated entirely, and a simple reference counting scheme could be implemented to detect termination of all codeblock continuations. If the other uses for signals could be handled in a different way, this reference counting optimization could save instructions and frame slots. This is a matter for additional study.

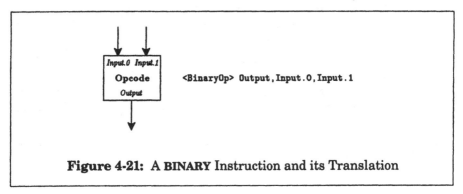

Figure 4-21: A BINARY Instruction and its Translation

Unary and binary instructions (arithmetic, logicals, relationals) expand by a simple rule: generate a machine instruction with the same opcode as the graph instruction, mapping input arcs to input frame slots, registers, or literals, and the output arc to the output frame slot or register (Figure 4-21).

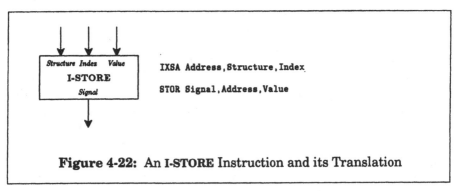

Figure 4-22: An I-STORE Instruction and its Translation

Recall that during program graph rewriting, all references to arrays, strings, tuples, and CONSes were simplified to I-FETCH and I-STORE. The translations of these to machine graph instructions are similar but not symmetric. The reason is, quite simply, that an indexed I-FETCH fits neatly into a three-address format while an indexed I-STORE does not. Hence, I-FETCHes are translated to single LOAD instructions, while I-STOREs are translated into a two-instruction suite: Index Structure Address (IXSA) followed by STOR (Figure 4-22)[40].

The IF encapsulator represents both an opportunity and an obstacle. The advantages of having the entire IF and its enclosed instructions within a single SQ are significant, c.f., myriad SWITCH instructions in the TTDA. The biggest obstacle is in the firing semantics of the IF. As defined by the rewrite rules, IF is necessarily nonstrict. This is perfectly clear when IF is expanded to its lowest level form (SWITCHes and MERGEs).

In order to reap the benefits of IF as an aggregate, it must be interpreted as a strict operation. Traub has demonstrated plausible, if contorted, instances of IF which are inherently non-sequential, i.e., the order of instruction execution both inside and outside the IF depends on program input. Such non-sequential instances of IF can potentially be recognized by cycles through the IF in the graph. For the sake of the present work, it was decided to compile IFs as if they were strict and to explicitly rewrite non-sequential IFs into their lower-level, i.e., SWITCH based, representations.

Strict IFs are easily translated. The predicate is evaluated and a conditional branch around the recursively expanded THEN basic block is taken. At the end of the THEN code, an unconditional branch is inserted to redirect the flow of control to the end of the ELSE block. See Figure 4-23.

Several assumptions are made in defining the expansion of LOOP encapsulators. As in the case of IF, the encapsulator is assumed to be strict in all of its arguments. Further, as in the TTDA, each codeblock is assumed to contain at most one LOOP. LOOP instances are restricted to execute on a single processor, unlike the TTDA which permits mapping of iterations

---

[40]In general, such multi-instruction suites benefit by having intermediate results stored in registers instead of frame slots. However, it is not always possible to do so when the suite may suspend at some point after the first instruction. This concern can be resolved at compile time by using registers for intermediates when the compiler can prove that such suspensions will not occur and frame slots otherwise. In the example, a register can be used for *Address* if and only if the access to *Value* is provably nonsuspensive.

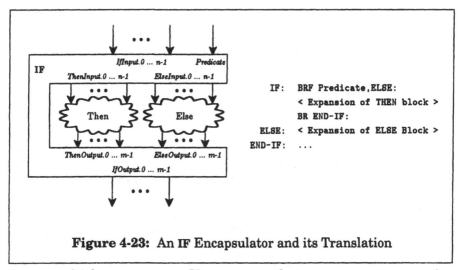

Figure 4-23: An **IF** Encapsulator and its Translation

across multiple processors. However, on that processor, K successive iterations may be active concurrently. In the event that there is inter-iteration parallelism in the program, this provides an additional source of work for hiding long-latency operations. In the frequent case of nested loops, K-unfolding of the the outer loop will allow K initiations of the next-innermore loop which are candidates for initiation on up to K processors, and so on. The argument also holds for loops which contain procedure invocations in either their predicate or body[41].

Figure 4-24 gives the overall structure of **LOOP** translation. The wide arrows represent control flow within the **LOOP** SQ while thin arrows denote data dependences. **LOOP**s are translated as a sequence of instructions within a single SQ. This instruction sequence may fork subordinate SQ's within the predicate and body per MDS, but the computation of such SQ's is constrained to complete prior to termination of a given iteration.

---

[41]Experience with the TTDA has demonstrated the importance of unraveling in exploiting the parallelism inherent in a program. On the hybrid model, this argument is equally true. While a number of different translations are possible, the chosen one demonstrates the hybrid model's ability to permit parallel execution of successive iterations in a general way. While the technique does not map iterations across processors, the fact that each instance of an inner loop represents a separate invocation (potentially on a different processor) still permits a substantial multiplicative effect on available parallelism. Other compilation techniques can be used to support loop spreading without changes to the model. These are not investigated here but rather are identified as an opportunity for future work.

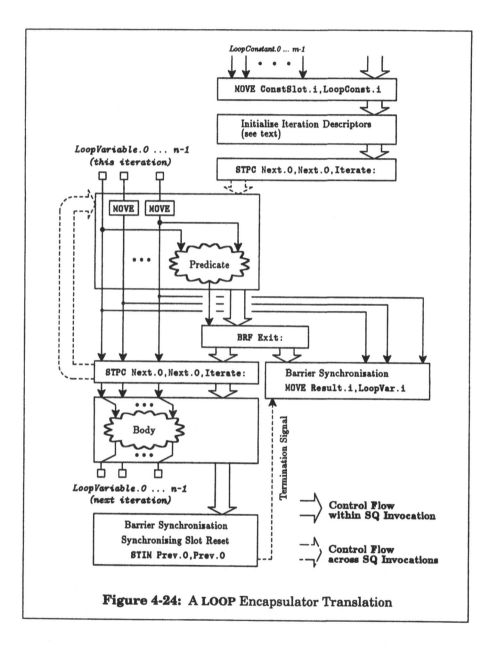

Figure 4-24: A LOOP Encapsulator Translation

- Loop constants are stored in the frame's constant area. For an inner loop, putting constants into the constant area is a side-effect of the codeblock invocation — the constant area is part of the argument area (see Section 4.3). For an outer loop, however, the arc-carried constants must be explicitly stored in the constant area. In both cases, references to constants can be nonsuspensive because no predicate or body instructions may execute until storage of constants is complete.

- *ITERATION-DESCRIPTOR*s are initialized for each of the K iteration areas in the frame. An iteration area is a block of linearly addressed frame slots as described in Section 4.3. The first slot of each area holds the iteration descriptor (*ID*) for that area (Section 3.2). The procedure is described below.

- The first iteration is started (described below).

- The predicate is evaluated.

- A conditional branch is taken to the loop epilog code if the predicate is **FALSE**, otherwise,

- The next iteration is triggered.

- The body is evaluated.

- A barrier synchronization is performed on the termination of all subordinate SQ's in the predicate and body, if there are any. Note that the initiation of the next iteration is independent of this barrier.

- Synchronizing slots are reset so that the iteration area can be reused.

- Termination of the iteration is signalled.

An iteration consists of the evaluation of the predicate and the subsequent evaluation of either the body or the loop epilog. Starting a given iteration requires the coincidence of three separate events:

1. CONTROL FLOW: The previous iteration has computed a **TRUE** predicate (call this $CNTL_i$), and

2. RECYCLING: The i-Kth iteration has terminated, thereby making the $i \bmod K$th iteration area available for re-use (call this $RECYC_{i\text{-}K}$), and

3. IMPORTATION: The i-K+1st iteration has indicated that its loop variables have been consumed, thereby permitting the slots in which they reside to be re-written (call this $IMPT_{i\text{-}k+1}$).

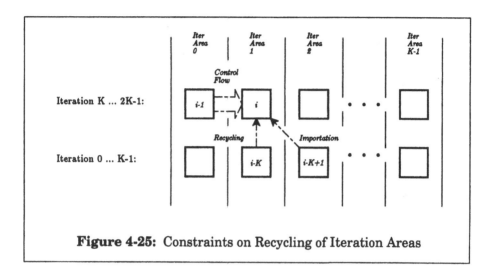

Figure 4-25: Constraints on Recycling of Iteration Areas

This is depicted in Figure 4-25. It is straightforward to show that, of these conditions, the second is a necessary consequence of the first and third.

Theorem 4-15: For any iteration i, the necessary and sufficient conditions for starting iteration i (INVOKE$_i$) are CNTL$_{i-1}$ and IMPT$_{i-K+1}$, or simply

$$\forall\, i,\ \text{INVOKE}_i \Leftrightarrow \text{CNTL}_{i-1} \wedge \text{IMPT}_{i-K+1} \qquad [1]$$

Given: The invocation condition as stated above,

$$\forall\, i,\ \text{INVOKE}_i \Leftrightarrow \text{CNTL}_{i-1} \wedge \text{IMPT}_{i-K+1} \wedge \text{RECYC}_{i-k} \quad [2]$$

Assume: The recycling and importation conditions are logically separate. However, in general, freeing the loop variable slots prior to iteration termination implies explicit copying of the variables out of these slots. It is assumed that there is little, if any, benefit in doing this and that it is reasonable to assume that both conditions are equivalent, *i.e.*,

$$\forall\, i,\ \text{RECYC}_i \Leftrightarrow \text{IMPT}_i \qquad [3]$$

Moreover, since predicate evaluation for a given iteration implies that the iteration must have been invoked,

$$\forall\, i,\ \text{CNTL}_i \Rightarrow \text{INVOKE}_i \qquad [4]$$

Proof Idea: At the point of invocation $INVOKE_i$, the condition $RECYC_{i \cdot K}$ can be deduced. In the proof below, the universal quantifiers have been dropped but are implicit.

Proof: ($\Leftarrow$)

$CNTL_{i-1} \wedge IMPT_{i \cdot K+1}$	antecedent
$CNTL_{i-1} \wedge IMPT_{i \cdot K+1} \Rightarrow INVOKE_{i-1} \wedge IMPT_{i \cdot K+1}$	by [4]
$INVOKE_{i-1} \wedge IMPT_{i \cdot K+1}$	$P \wedge (\sim P \vee Q)$
$INVOKE_{i-1} \Leftrightarrow CNTL_{i-2} \wedge IMPT_{i \cdot k} \wedge RECYC_{i \cdot k-1}$	by [2]
$CNTL_{i-2} \wedge IMPT_{i \cdot K} \wedge RECYC_{i \cdot K-1} \wedge IMPT_{i \cdot K+1}$	substitutivity
$IMPT_{i \cdot k}$	selection
$RECYC_{i \cdot k}$	by [3]
$CNTL_{i-1} \wedge IMPT_{i \cdot K+1} \wedge RECYC_{i \cdot k}$	$\wedge$ antecedent
$INVOKE_i$	by [2]

Proof: ($\Rightarrow$)

$INVOKE_i$	antecedent
$CNTL_{i-1} \wedge IMPT_{i \cdot K+1} \wedge RECYC_{i \cdot k}$	by [2]
$CNTL_{i-1} \wedge IMPT_{i \cdot K+1}$	selection

$\square$

It is now relatively easy to understand the function of the **STPC** and **STIM** machine ops. **STPC** (SeT Program Counter) signals the $CNTL_i$ condition, meaning that the predicate has evaluated to **TRUE** in iteration i. It is represented as a boolean flag in the iteration descriptor for iteration area $i+1 \bmod K$. The **STIM** (SeT IMport flag) op signals $IMPT_i$, meaning that iteration i has ended and that no further access to the loop variables for that iteration will be made. It is represented as a boolean flag in the descriptor for iteration $i-1 \bmod K$.

Termination of an iteration implies that all *BodyOutput.n* inputs to the **LOOP** have produced results and that subordinate SQ's triggered in the process have terminated. The former condition is subsumed by the latter and that all predicate and/or body instructions in the **LOOP**'s SQ have executed (a simple assertion to make based on the program counter). Thus, the only problem is to detect SQ termination. For this, an iteration area slot is allocated per subordinate SQ (there may be none), and each subordinate is amended to store into this slot upon termination. In the **LOOP**'s SQ, then, it is only necessary to probe (suspensively) these slots with **TSTN** ops as appropriate.

Prior to issuing the STIM, signalling the end of the iteration, all slots in
the iteration area which are used for explicit synchronization (*i.e.*, those
which will be read suspensively) must be reset[42]. The iteration area slots
which must be reset are exactly the following:

- The loop variables. These synchronize production of values in
  iteration i and consumption in iteration $i+1$.

- Inputs to subordinate SQ's. These synchronize the action of
  threads of computation which go on in parallel with the LOOP
  SQ.

- *BodyOutput.n* inputs to the LOOP which are dynamic arcs.

An interesting optimization results if loop variables are constrained in
their fanout such that

- within the body of the current iteration they have no sinks
  (*e.g.*, a *next*ified variable, in Id parlance, used on the right
  hand side in a loop body).

- within the predicate of the next iteration they have but a
  single sink, or, within the predicate they have no sink but
  within the body they have but a single sink.

Under these conditions, it is possible to use the nonsticky addressing mode
on the single predicate sink or the single body sink, as appropriate, to obviate the need for explicitly resetting the slot. A tradeoff exists in that
loop variables which do not satisfy the constraints can be transformed into
ones that do, but the cost of doing so (essentially introducing MOVE instructions as identities so as to guarantee unity fanout) in some cases out-
weighs the benefit of eliminating explicit RSTNs.

For other slots requiring reset, unity fanout implies that the resetting can
always be done by the reader. Further, non-unity fanout within a single

---

[42]In models such as Monsoon [46], slots are self-cleaning in that they are associated
with instructions in a graph which self-clean at the abstract interpreter level. Slots in
the hybrid model are instead associated with instruction outputs with unrestricted
fanout, the readers of which may be in different SQ's. In general, then, no reader of any
slot may be labeled *a priori* as the last reader, because the readers are at best partially
ordered. In the body of a codeblock (outside of any LOOP), slots are written at most
once, and cleanup is implicit in the process of frame allocation and deallocation. It is
only within a LOOP that the issue of slot-resetting arises.

SQ can be similarly optimized by making the last reader perform the non-sticky reference.

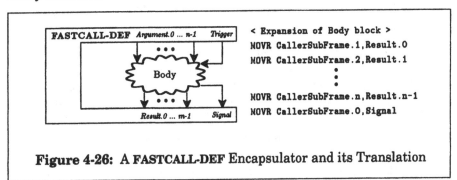

Figure 4-26: A **FASTCALL-DEF** Encapsulator and its Translation

FASTCALL-DEF implements the invoked half of basic procedure linkage[43]. It is responsible for triggering the enclosed codeblock, returning the codeblock results to the invoker, and finally sending a termination signal. This is implemented in a straightforward fashion by expanding the body of the **FASTCALL-DEF** and then generating suspensive Move Remote (**MOVR**) instructions for each result. The procedure linkage protocol mandates the return of a signal — if the codeblock generates one, it is returned to the invoker via a suspensive **MOVR**. If no signal is generated, a dummy signal is sent after the results have been sent. See Figure 4-26.

FASTCALL-APPLY-INITIATE implements the *invoker* part of basic procedure linkage[44]. It is responsible for allocating a fresh context and sending the arguments to the new frame.

The frame descriptor (*FD*) for *Codeblock* is allocated and stored in the *InvokedContext* frame slot. A procedure call subframe for the returned *signal* and the *result*(s) has already been allocated during frame slot assignment, starting at the *signal* slot (see section 4.3). This slot number is

---

[43]Recall that **DEF** argument chain unpacking is, at this point, handled by graph instructions which are separate from the **FASTCALL-DEF**.

[44]Recall that **APPLY** and **DIRECT-APPLY** have been re-written by this point into instances of **FASTCALL-APPLY**, which subsequently get rewritten into instances of **FASTCALL-APPLY-INITIATE** and one other instruction which disposes of the called context.

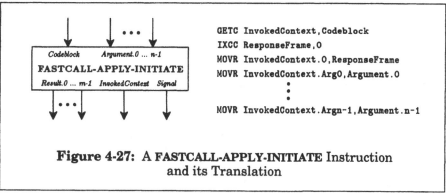

Figure 4-27: A **FASTCALL-APPLY-INITIATE** Instruction
and its Translation

added to the current context (frame descriptor), yielding a new frame descriptor which points to the procedure call subframe. This descriptor (stored in a register) is forwarded to the 0th slot of the invoked frame (per section 4.3) by a **MOVR** instruction. The arguments are likewise forwarded to the appropriate argument slots by **MOVR** instructions. See Figure 4-27.

Summary. This section has presented the issues which surround the translation of macro-expanded graphs into partitioned machine code, and a set of methods for handling them. Significant among the issues are the dichotomy of synchronization methods, implicit and explicit, and the optimizations which are made possible thereby.

It is clear that this dichotomy, if it is to be used to advantage, makes the task of code generation significantly harder than in the TTDA case and, arguably, than in the von Neumann case. This is because both paradigms (read: both sets of problems) are present in the hybrid model.

The techniques developed in this study demonstrate the benefit of keeping the issues of partitioning and operand addressing separate from the semantics of code generation. Here, both partitioning and operand addressing are done algorithmically, and the specification of these algorithms is completely independent of the specification of graph instruction translations. At a pragmatic level, this made experimentation with the instruction set possible. At a higher level, it demonstrates that the complexity of the hybrid model is entirely manageable within a traditional compiler mind set.

Optimizer

Two types of SQ structural optimization are performed on the codeblock after all instructions have been translated.

Null SQ Elimination. The first of these optimizations strips out degenerate SQ's which are a consequence of the implementation of MDS. Because abstract translation is specified separately from the mechanism of allocating and installing triggers for SQ's, it occasionally the case that an SQ shell is eagerly created into which no machine instructions are actually generated. Here, a distinction is made between instructions which trigger SQ's and all others. The latter instructions are called LIVE INSTRUCTIONS. A null SQ is defined as one with no live instructions. For each null SQ, the SQ and its trigger (which appears in some other SQ) can be removed. This will remove both the truly empty SQ's and those which merely contain triggers for other SQ's. In the latter case, the triggers are moved backwards toward the distinguished SQ until a non-null SQ is found[45]. Suppose, for example, non-null SQ A triggers SQ B. B contains no instructions — only a trigger to C. Therefore, B can be eliminated, as can be the trigger for B which appears in A. In its place, the trigger for C is installed.

Tail Call Elimination. For all the cases where SQ A ends with a trigger to SQ B, a new SQ is formed by appending B to the end of A.

It is easily shown that neither of these transformations corrupt the assertions previously made about the introduction of cycles as a function of the partitioning.

Assembler

The final phase in the compilation is the ASSEMBLER, which translates the partitioned machine instructions into actual PML code. At this stage, the set of partitioned machine instructions is represented as a set of instruction lists, one per SQ. The distinguished SQ is so marked. The output file format consists of some codeblock property information (*e.g.*, number of base and iteration frame slots to be allocated upon invocation) followed by

---

[45]This process is guaranteed to succeed because all triggers are traceable to the distinguished SQ, and the distinguished SQ is always non-null.

the contents of the SQ's, distinguished first[46]

As SQ's are written, triggers are transformed into Continue (**CNTN**) instructions. **CNTN**, when executed, causes a new continuation to be formed and executed. By definition, all non-constant arcs which are input to an SQ imply synchronization. Therefore, the most common situation is that the first instruction of the SQ, when executed, makes a suspensive reference to one or more frame slots. Consider the reference to the very first slot. If it is *full*, instruction execution proceeds normally. If it is *empty*, the newly-created continuation will immediately suspend.

An important optimization of this relies on the fact that the **CNTN** instruction which creates the continuation itself references no frame slots. A variant on this instruction, Continue and Test (**CNTT**), can test exactly one frame slot for the presence or absence of a value. **CNTT** creates a continuation, and tests this slot. When a value is present, the continuation is scheduled for execution just as in the case of **CNTN**. If no value is present, the continuation is immediately put into the *suspended* state, potentially saving an explicit suspension. For each trigger, the assembler is responsible for determining which frame slot the denoted SQ will test first and for manufacturing an appropriate **CNTT** instruction.

4.4 SUMMARY

In this Chapter, the structure, instructions and manipulated data types of the dataflow program graph have been reviewed. Dataflow program graphs are made up of both simple instructions and encapsulators, the latter capturing notions of iteration, conditional execution, and procedure linkage.

Also in this Chapter, the method of generating code under the new parallel machine language model has been presented in detail. Key problems in performing the translation include keeping the abstract translation of instructions separate from the issues of partitioning. The partitioning method and its properties have been formally presented.

---

[46]Output files are encoded in CIOBL, a system-independent format which is described in [57].

Chapter Five

Analysis

This chapter presents experimental results from the first set of emulation studies of the hybrid architecture along with a comparison to similar results from studies of the TTDA. Section 5.1 considers the behavior of a collection of benchmark programs as compiled for the hybrid architecture and as executed by the idealized machine. The results reflect the characteristics of the programs subject to the hybrid partitioning constraints. A comparison is made to the TTDA which shows how the hybrid's less powerful instructions can be used in place of TTDA instructions with little change in dynamic instruction counts. Also in this section, the costs and benefits of dynamic loop unfolding are studied. Section 5.2 examines the behavior of the realistic model using these same benchmark programs. The costs of aborted instructions (due to synchronization tests which fail) and multi-ported access to the local memory are considered. Data cache effectiveness is studied.

5.1 IDEALIZED MODEL

Static and dynamic characteristics of a number of small benchmark programs are now considered using the hybrid code generator and an implementation of an idealized model interpreter. The purpose is to better understand the effects of partitioning dataflow graphs, and to establish a baseline of performance for studies to be done on the realistic model. In the course of these experiments, comparisons are made to the TTDA. These comparisons come from executing exactly the same programs (same source code files, actually) on the GITA[47] interpreter. It is shown that, for

---

[47]GITA, or the Graph Interpreter for the Tagged-token Architecture, was developed by Arvind's group at MIT for analyzing the behavior of programs under the TTDA paradigm. Principal contributors to GITA were Ken Traub, David Culler, and Dinarte Morais. By some strange coincidence, *Gita* is also Arvind's wife's name.

a number of cases, it does indeed happen that the hybrid model executes fewer instructions (and thereby fewer cycles) than the TTDA.

Static Statistics

A number of example programs[48] have been chosen to characterize this architecture. This section presents the static characteristics of a cross-section of these programs, chosen according to the architectural features which they exercise. The table gives the total static instruction count, the total number of SQ's, length of shortest and longest SQ's, and the mean SQ length.

Table 5-1: Static Characteristics					
Codeblock	Instrs	SQ's	Shortest	Longest	Mean
ABS	4	2	1	3	2.00
AND	6	3	1	4	2.00
ARRAY	7	3	1	4	2.33
+	6	3	1	4	2.00
EXPRESSION	15	7	1	7	2.14
FIB	31	6	2	19	5.17
FOR_LOOP	37	4	2	23	9.25
IF_EXPR	22	5	1	9	4.40
MM	94	11	1	29	8.55
MM-0	59	8	1	39	7.37
MM-0-0	47	7	1	29	6.71
MERGESORT	11	3	2	5	3.67
MERGESORT-DIVIDE-0-0	95	19	1	20	5.00
MERGESORT-MERGE-0-0	108	20	1	30	5.40
MERGESORT-SORT-0-0	89	16	1	27	5.56
ATAN	130	7	1	45	18.57
COS	50	2	12	38	25.00
LOG	41	2	10	31	20.50
SIN	49	2	12	37	24.50
SQRT	63	2	9	54	31.50
MULTIWAVE	68	10	1	32	6.80
WAVEFRONT	67	11	1	15	6.09
WAVEFRONT-0	56	7	1	31	8.00
WAVEFRONT-0-0	53	7	1	34	7.57
WAVEFRONT-1	51	8	1	33	6.37

Procedures from the first group were taken from the Id Basic Library, a set of very short, separately compiled procedures. The instruction count is attributable primarily to parameter passing overhead. Recall that ar-

---

[48]These programs were taken from the ID Library and were not created by the author. Most, if not all, of these are attributable to Rishiyur Nikhil and Ken Traub.

guments to a procedure are treated as dynamic synchronized arcs. Hence, the number of SQ's will be bounded from below by one (the distinguished SQ) plus the number of arguments. Hence, the monadic function ABS is made up of two SQ's, while the dyadic AND is made up of three. The number of instructions is similarly bounded from below: there will be one instruction to trigger each SQ other than the distinguished one, one instruction to return the termination signal, one instruction for each result value, plus the body of the function. In the case of ABS, there is one result and one instruction (**ABS**) in the body. Although AND has a single-instruction body, the counts reflect the addition of another SQ which conditionally unpacks the argument chain in the case that **DIRECT-APPLY** linkage is not used. Statically, two additional instructions are added (one to trigger the extra SQ, and one instruction in that SQ to read the first argument in the chain). Dynamically, however, the situation is a bit different as discussed below. The dynamic instruction count depends on the method of invocation — if **DIRECT-APPLY** is used, the dynamic instruction count will be less than the static figure.

Procedures in the next group are slightly more complex. The simplest procedure is EXPRESSION, which evaluates b^2-4ac. Its longest SQ is the distinguished one which triggers five other SQ's, then synchronizes on the availability of the result, returns it, and then returns a signal. A more elaborate procedure is IF_EXPR, which compares two numbers and then returns a tuple consisting of the larger number followed by the difference between the two numbers. At the other end of the spectrum are recursive Fibonacci (FIB) and triply-nested loops in matrix multiplication (MM). Because no codeblock may contain more than one loop, MM is split by the compiler into three codeblocks — one for the main procedure and outermost loop, and one each for the remaining two loops. The interface to these two subordinate codeblocks is via the **FASTCALL** protocol. The next group represents the codeblocks for MERGESORT which operate on lists. As in the case of the previous group, procedures which invoke subordinate codeblocks (either nested loops or procedures) and/or involve the manipulation of structures (a dynamic arc per reference) have a significant number of SQ's and a correspondingly short mean SQ length.

The next group is taken from the Id Transcendental Library. These procedures are interesting in that they involve no loops but rather the evaluation of a Maclaurin series expansion as a large expression. Because there are no subordinate codeblocks and no I-structures, there is a higher ratio of computational instructions to dynamic arcs, resulting in fewer, longer SQ's.

WaveFront and MultiWave are also included, and are discussed below.

Dynamic Characteristics

Table 5-2: Dynamic Characteristics, $K=2$							
Codeblock	Instrs	Critical Path	Aborts	% Aborts	Arith	% Arith	Run Length
ABS 1	4	4	1	25.00	1	25.00	1.3
AND $T $T	5	5	1	20.00	1	20.00	1.7
ARRAY $<0 10>	7	8	1	14.29	0	0	1.7
+ 1 2	5	5	1	20.00	1	20.00	1.7
EXPRESSION 1 2 3	11	8	1	9.09	4	36.36	1.8
FIB 10	3,265	187	265	8.12	441	13.51	3.4
FOR_LOOP 1000	7,030	7,028	1	0.01	3,001	42.69	7.0
IF_EXPR 1 2	17	11	3	17.65	2	11.76	2.4
MM 10x10	23,569	21,924	2,432	10.32	4,352	18.46	3.7
MERGESORT <20..1>	16,053	2,910	3,104	19.34	430	2.68	2.2
ATAN 0.1 1	110	70	5	4.55	22	20.00	10.0
COS 0.1	43	42	1	2.33	23	53.49	14.3
LOG 0.1	34	32	1	2.94	17	50.00	11.3
SIN 0.1	42	41	1	2.38	21	50.00	14.0
SQRT 0.1	51	49	1	1.96	23	45.10	17.0
MULTIWAVE 15x15x2	12,769	5,694	538	4.21	2,787	21.83	5.4
WAVEFRONT 15x15	5,894	5,030	262	4.45	1,294	21.95	5.6

Now, the example programs are analyzed using an idealized mode emulator for the hybrid architecture. As part of the emulation, a number of statistics are gathered, and a subset of these are presented in the table. They are

- INSTRUCTION COUNT: Each successfully-executed instruction is counted. Aborted instructions (those which do not complete due to a synchronization blockage) are not counted.

- CRITICAL PATH: Given a notion of one instruction executing in unit time and a time axis with zero corresponding to the initiation of the procedure, this is the least time after which the parallelism profile is identically zero[49].

- ABORTS: Each aborted instruction is counted — if an instruc-

---

[49]This definition is due to Arvind.

tion aborts more than once (*e.g.*, two synchronizing input operands), it is so counted. Aborts are also expressed as a percentage of Instruction Count. While it has never happened in practice, it is possible to have a value greater than 100% here.

- ARITHMETIC INSTRUCTIONS: Each successful ALU operation (arithmetic, logical, relational) is counted — the value is also expressed as a percentage of the Instruction Count.

- RUN LENGTH: A measure of the mean time between context switches (see Section 4.2).

Assumption. It is assumed that multiple suspended reads against a single frame slot are rare. This assumption is borne out by the relatively low percentage of aborted instructions — each abort causes a suspension against a slot. Given a low percentage of total aborts, the probability of multiple, simultaneous suspensions against a single slot is correspondingly low. Hence, multiple suspensions are "stored" in a single slot in the same way a single suspension is.

The statistics gathered establish a best case baseline for additional analysis in later sections. To that end, K has been set to its minimum value of two. In a later section, the effect of K will be analyzed in some depth.

Analysis. In the first group of benchmarks, the dynamic cost of procedure invocation is demonstrated. As expected, the instruction count for monadic procedures matches the static instruction count (*c.f.*, the Static table), while procedures with more than one argument show fewer dynamic instructions[50]. Arithmetic counts correspond to the useful instruction in the body. Abort percentages are artificially high only because the number of instructions is so low. Mean run length is correspondingly short.

In the second group, FOR_LOOP shows a mean run length of 7.0. The loop itself is 7 instructions long, and because inter-iteration arcs are treated as dynamic, each inner loop instance is a separate SQ invocation. Thus, a sequence break occurs between iterations. By contrast, the run length in MM (matrix multiplication) is shorter because the inner loop

---

[50]The interpreter uses the **DIRECT-APPLY** protocol for invocation at top level.

body contains embedded dynamic arcs (two **I-FETCH** instructions for the elements being multiplied) and, consequently, several short SQ's instead of a single, longer one. MM will be revisited shortly when the cost of K-unfolding is studied.

As expected, the trigonometric procedures are very efficient: because there are no embedded procedure calls, inner loops, or structures, there are no internal dynamic arcs. Further, these routines are all monadic (except ATAN). The resulting partitioning maps all instructions into the same dependence set, and no dynamic synchronizations save references to the argument are done[51].

The Cost of K-Unfolding. The ability to unfold successive iterations of a loop has significant value in the dataflow environment for exposing parallelism. In the hybrid case, the motivation is similar, but given that no mechanism is provided at the hardware level for spreading iterations of a single loop across processors[52], there is little benefit to unfolding inner loops in some cases. Moreover, the cost of inner loop unfolding is noteworthy, particularly for simple inner loops where the loop body is the size of the iteration set-up code, or nearly so.

Unlike the TTDA scheme, there is a clear cost in the hybrid model for loop unfolding in terms of additional synchronization instructions and frame area. This cost scales with K. Hence, for any one program instance, there must be some optimum value of K which balances exposed parallelism against execution of overhead instructions.

The first set of matrix multiplications (MM) was chosen specifically to show the effects of large values of K on inner loop unfoldings. The table shows, as a function of the number of concurrent iterations (Loops) and K (K=Loops+1), the instruction counts, the critical path, and the average

---

[51]Although possible, the existing code generator does not optimize the case of multiple references to a dynamic arc's slot within the same SQ. All references are coded as synchronizing. Dynamically, only one suspension can actually take place for a given SQ / operand pair. However, the instruction dispatcher will treat each such reference as potentially suspensive, admitting context swapping. Such an optimization is worthwhile and relatively straightforward to implement.

[52]It is possible to do limited loop spreading by compiling specifically for it.

Table 5-3: MM, Various Unfoldings				
Loops	K	Instrs	Critical Path	Average Parallelism
1	2	23,569	21,924	1.1
2	3	24,017	3,864	6.2
10	11	27,601	576	47.9
16	17	30,289	648	46.7
1	2	23,569	21,924	1.1
2	3	23,617	5,739	4.1
3	4	23,665	3,697	6.4
4	5	23,713	2,221	10.7
5	6	23,761	1,215	19.6
6	7	23,809	1,186	20.1
7	8	23,857	1,157	20.6
8	9	23,905	1,128	21.2
9	10	23,953	1,099	21.8
10	11	24,001	615	39.0
11	12	24,049	623	38.6
12	13	24,097	631	38.2
13	14	24,145	639	37.8
14	15	24,193	647	37.4
15	16	24,241	655	37.0
16	17	24,289	663	36.6

parallelism (instruction count divided by critical path) for a 10×10 example. In all cases, the run length was constant at 3.7, and the number of arithmetic operations was 4,352.

As was expected, the cost of increasing K by 1 is on the order of $4n^2$, or 400: the difference in instruction count between two runs whose K's differ by one is 448 (higher-order effects account for the remainder of the instructions, e.g., $4n$ overhead instructions for the n middle loops). However, over the range where K is increasing toward n, the change in K has a profound effect on the critical path and the average parallelism. The optimal value for this case occurs with ten concurrent iterations, or K=11. Beyond this point, the increasing time spent in overhead instructions for each inner loop instance causes an increase in critical path time. The run length also increases, but only for pathological reasons — the loop initialization code is a tight, unsynchronizing loop dependent upon the value of K. As K increases, this loop dominates the computation, and the mean run length tends toward the dynamic length of this loop[53].

---

[53]David Culler has pointed out an interesting optimization, not explored in this work, of spawning a separate SQ to perform initialization of the iteration descriptors for each of the K iteration areas. This would result in a nearly trivial increase in instruction count, but would have a very noticeable effect of shortening the critical path time.

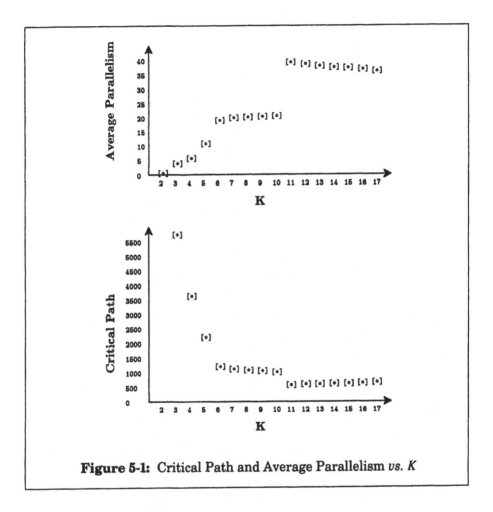

Figure 5-1: Critical Path and Average Parallelism *vs. K*

The second set of matrix multiplications shows an interesting effect. In this case, the outer and middle loops were *K*-unfolded, but the inner loops were prohibited from unfolding (*i.e., K*=2). Despite this, the average parallelism is on the same order, and the run length is unchanged. Moreover, the incremental cost of unfolding has been dramatically reduced from 448 to 48. Thus, the total number of instructions is a much weaker function of *K*. Deciding how and when to unfold loops is a difficult problem which is explored by Culler in his dissertation [20].

The critical path and average parallelism values show some interesting discontinuities which are better visualized with the aid of Figure 5-1. For

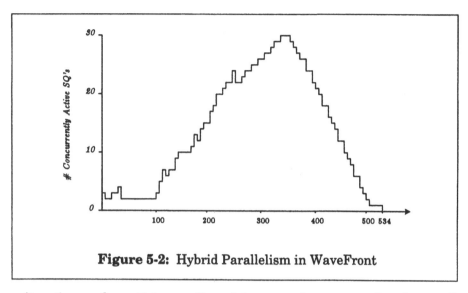

Figure 5-2: Hybrid Parallelism in WaveFront

n iterations, where $K-1$ are allowed to proceed concurrently, there will necessarily be $\lceil \frac{n}{K-1} \rceil$ sequentialized sets of iterations. It is this nonlinearity which gives rise to the discontinuities.

Just as in a dynamic dataflow machine, the benefits of loop unfolding can be exploited in the hybrid regime. The costs can be managed at compile and/or load times in that the unfolding mechanism is dynamic and is simply controlled by the invocation constant K. Costs are a weak function of K, but the effect for nested loops is necessarily multiplicative.

WaveFront Revisited

Table 5-4: 15x15 WaveFront Dynamics								
Codeblock	Instrs	Critical Path	Aborts	% Aborts	Arith	% Arith	Run Length	Average Parallelism
MultiWave, K=2	12,769	5,694	538	4.21	2,787	21.83	5.4	2.2
MultiWave, K=16	14,729	679	1,063	7.22	2,787	18.92	5.1	21.7
WaveFront, K=2	5,894	5,030	262	4.45	1,294	21.95	5.6	1.2
WaveFront, K=16	6,846	534	533	7.79	1,294	18.90	5.1	12.8

In motivating this architecture, three forms of parallelism were described using the WaveFront example. An idealized parallelism profile was presented for WaveFront and its companion program MultiWave. It was argued that von Neumann machines were inherently incapable of exploiting all three forms, and that hardware changes were required to support

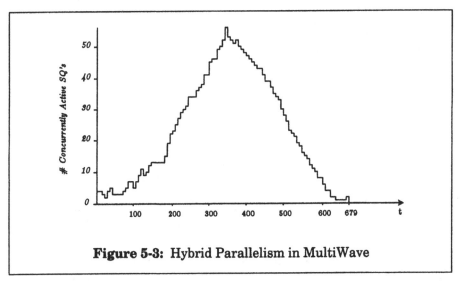

Figure 5-3: Hybrid Parallelism in MultiWave

the necessary fine-grained synchronization. The hybrid model was developed in response to the challenge of keeping the von Neumann machine's ability to mask latency using expression level parallelism and instruction reordering (a big improvement in locality over a dataflow machine) while simultaneously exploiting the other two kinds of parallelism.

Figure 5-2 shows the parallelism profile which results from executing the WaveFront example under the idealized hybrid model. The vertical axis represents the number of concurrently executable SQ's as a function of time (*c.f.*, Figure 2-4, p. 44). Figure 5-3 shows two iterations of the MultiWave example, also under ideal assumptions (*c.f.*, Figure 2-5a, p. 46). As is obvious from the figures, the hybrid model is capable of exploiting the parallelism inherent in this application by virtue of the fine-grained synchronization mechanisms. Details of these experiments are shown in the table. Full unfolding of outer and inner loops was performed for the $K=16$ cases. The increase of average parallelism as K is scaled to its optimum value is not nearly so dramatic as in the matrix multiplication case simply because the algorithmic parallelism is $O(n)$ *vs.* $O(n^3)$ for matrix multiplication.

Power of a Hybrid Instruction

Assuming all other things equal, *e.g.*, the opcode set, hybrid instructions are strictly less powerful than TTDA instructions (*viz.*, forking). An interesting question, as alluded to earlier, is whether the full generality of TTDA instructions is used frequently or infrequently. By using the identical dataflow program graphs in generating code for both the TTDA and the hybrid machine, it has been possible to study this question in some detail.

Table 5-5: Comparison of Hybrid and TTDA				
Codeblock	Hybrid Instrs	Critical Path	TTDA Instrs	Critical Path
ABS 1	4	4	9	5
AND $T $T	5	5	9	5
ARRAY $<0 10>	7	8	11	6
+ 1 2	5	5	9	5
EXPRESSION 1 2 3	11	8	13	7
FIB 10	3,265	187	3,708	115
FOR_LOOP 1000	7,030	7,028	10,023	6,011
IF_EXPR 1 2	17	11	18	9
MM 10x10	23,569	21,924	20,118	11,228
MERGESORT <20..1>	16,053	2,910	17,549	1,280
ATAN 0.1 1	110	70	96	27
COS 0.1	43	42	35	24
LOG 0.1	34	32	30	20
SIN 0.1	42	41	33	22
SQRT 0.1	51	49	41	27
MULTIWAVE 15x15x2	12,769	5,694	9,584	2,701
WAVEFRONT 15x15	5,894	5,030	4,523	2,477

The Table shows dynamic instruction counts for the benchmark programs as executed on both the hybrid machine and on the TTDA using the same source program for both[54,55]. The counts do not favor either architecture but rather show that, for a variety of program types, instruction counts are comparable to first order. If hybrid instructions are less powerful, how can this be?

---

[54]In neither case is the type of emulation model (idealized or not) relevant for instruction counts. Instruction counts do not vary across these models.

[55]Some care is needed in interpreting TTDA critical path numbers in that the GITA interpreter counts instructions, and instructions are not cycles in the strict sense, *e.g.*, for pipeline depth greater than one. The hybrid interpreter also counts instruction, but the assumption of instructions being cycles is more reasonably made.

One part of the answer lies in the reduced number of overhead operators in the hybrid code resulting from fewer independent threads. In the TTDA, termination detection is done via trees of IDENTITY instructions. The leaves of these trees are the instructions which otherwise produce no tokens, *e.g.*, STORE operations. In the hybrid model, it is only necessary to test for termination of the SQ in which such instructions reside. Hence, n STOREs in one SQ imply only one explicit synchronization operation instead of a binary tree of $n-1$ IDENTITY instructions.

Another part of the answer is elimination of the need to perform explicit fan-out of FETCHed values; the associated frame slots can simply be re-read. In the TTDA, however, FETCH operations can have only a single destination instruction. Multiple destinations imply the need for an IDENTITY instruction as the destination for the FETCH.

It is likely that the remainder is attributable to the fact that it does not in general take two hybrid instructions to displace a single TTDA instruction. There are many instances of TTDA instructions in typical programs where the full generality and power of the instruction is not being used in the sense that the hybrid partitioning strategy chooses to eliminate it rather than mimic it. In the hybrid model, parallelism is retained in the machine code only when dictated by dynamic arc constraints. According to this view, the remainder of the parallelism in TTDA code and its associated forking are superfluous.

In the next section, the effect of this reduced parallelism in terms of the hybrid machine's ability to tolerate latency is examined.

5.2 REALISTIC MODEL

In this section, the benchmark programs are used to characterize the realistic model. In particular, critical path time is evaluated as a function of data cache parameters, the number of processors, and communication latency. First, the matrix multiplication example is used to establish an operating point for the data cache. Using this, the remaining benchmarks are run with no cache, with the cache at the operating point, and with an infinite cache to demonstrate the robustness of the operating point. Then, the number of processors is allowed to vary. Finally, latency is introduced.

In the realistic emulator, codeblock invocations are assigned to a specific logical processor. At most one instruction may be executed at any given time on any given processor. Moreover, a one cycle time penalty is charged for each aborted instruction, and extra cycles are accrued for frame accesses above one per instruction in the absence of cache hits. Thus, an instruction making two frame references where one operand is found in the cache will take unit time, while the same instruction will take two time units when neither operand is found in the cache. Register accesses are considered to be free. The minimum communication latency L is one instruction time. This is charged against all packets formed by MOVR, LOAD, and STOR instructions.

I-Structures are handled by an idealized processor which services requests without imposing queue penalties. However, communication latency L also applies to the results returned by LOAD packets. Hence, in the best case, a LOAD will incur $2L$ units of latency in addition to the actual service time charged by the I-Structure processor (a minimum of one additional instruction time).

Cache Operating Point

In the realistic interpreter, each processor has a single data cache. All operand fetches are directed at the cache. Both successful fetches (hits) and unsuccessful fetches (misses) are counted. Hit rate is computed as the ratio of hits to accesses. The cache is organized as S sets, each with A associativity classes, and is referred to as an $S{\times}A$ cache. The denoted cache line is a single local memory word. The cache performs no prefetching, and ALU results are stored through to the local memory. Hence, writeback is never necessary. Mapping of local memory addresses into set addresses is done by simple hashing (exclusive-or folding) of the address.

The Table shows the effects of various cache organizations on the critical path time for a 5×5 matrix multiplication example, using a single processor, LIFO queueing, and $K{=}2$. For this example, an infinite cache results in a hit rate of 63.5% and a critical path time of 4,996[56]. The idealized hit rate of less than 100% is understandable because all references to the

---

[56]The difference between this value and the raw instruction count is attributable to nonzero latency which was not masked by parallel activity and to instruction aborts.

Table 5-6: Critical Path *vs.* Cache Parameters			
Cache	Critical Path	Hit Rate	Effective Hit
None	5,980	0	0
Infinite	4,996	63.5	100.0
1x1	5,475	26.2	41.3
2x1	5,261	33.4	52.6
4x1	5,184	41.2	64.9
8x1	5,105	48.1	75.7
16x1	5,080	53.4	84.1
32x1	5,014	58.7	92.4
64x1	5,005	60.3	95.0
128x1	5,000	61.6	97.0
256x1	4,997	62.7	98.7
1x2	5,474	28.3	44.6
2x2	5,066	42.7	67.2
4x2	5,057	51.1	80.5
8x2	5,022	56.6	89.1
16x2	5,007	60.1	94.6
32x2	4,998	61.9	97.5
64x2	4,996	62.5	98.4
128x2	4,996	63.0	99.2
1x4	5,061	43.5	68.5
2x4	5,046	53.7	84.6
4x4	5,013	57.9	91.2
8x4	5,000	61.6	97.0
16x4	4,998	62.1	97.8
32x4	4,996	63.2	99.5
64x4	4,996	63.4	99.8
1x8	5,034	56.5	89.0
2x8	5,005	58.6	92.3
4x8	4,999	61.9	97.5
8x8	4,999	62.1	97.8
16x8	4,996	63.4	99.8
32x8	4,996	63.4	99.8

cache are counted, not just those from successful instructions. Readers of unwritten slots will, by definition, cause cache misses no matter how big the cache is. Hence, it is useful to factor out this program-specific behavior by calculating an effective cache hit rate as the ratio of actual hit rate to ideal hit rate. This is shown in the table.

Run length was uniformly 3.7 in these experiments.

It is clear, at least with this simple example, that a fairly small, simple cache has a profound effect on eliminating the multiple frame access penalty. In the next section, the robustness of the 64x4 cache is tested with the other benchmark programs. This organization and size will be used for the remainder of the realistic mode experiments as the cache OPERATING POINT.

Cache Robustness

Table 5-7: Critical Path *vs.* Type of Cache						
Codeblock	No Cache	Infinite Cache	Hit Rate	64x4 Cache	Hit Rate	Effective Hit
ABS 1	7	6	12.5	6	12.5	100.0
AND $T $T	9	8	12.5	8	12.5	100.0
ARRAY $<0 10>	15	14	8.3	14	8.3	100.0
+ 1 2	9	8	12.5	8	12.5	100.0
EXPRESSION 1 2 3	18	15	31.2	15	31.2	100.0
FIB 10	4,501	4,059	55.0	4,059	54.4	98.9
FOR_LOOP 1000	9,037	7,033	99.9	7,033	99.9	100.0
IF_EXPR 1 2	25	21	58.3	21	58.3	100.0
MERGESORT <20..1>	23,252	20,858	48.6	20,956	45.6	93.8
ATAN 0.1 1	157	118	90.4	118	90.4	100.0
COS 0.1	61	45	90.9	45	90.9	100.0
LOG 0.1	52	36	80.8	36	80.8	100.0
SIN 0.1	59	44	90.3	44	90.3	100.0
SQRT 0.1	67	53	85.0	53	85.0	100.0
MULTIWAVE 15x15x2	17,739	13,861	70.3	13,870	70.0	99.6
WAVEFRONT 15x15	8,114	6,417	71.6	6,418	71.5	99.9
MULTIWAVE, K=16	20,137	15,773	70.3	15,784	69.1	98.3
WAVEFRONT, K=16	9,305	7,355	71.4	7,359	70.4	98.6

The table shows the performance of the other benchmark programs given the assumptions of no cache, an infinite cache, and a 64x4 cache. For the infinite and 64x4 cases, the actual hit rate is shown. The effective hit rate for the 64x4 cache is also calculated. In all but the last two runs, $K=2$. For most of the $K=2$ cases except Mergesort, the ratio of local memory space used to the 256 word capacity of the 64x4 cache was 1:1 or less. For the remaining three runs, the ratios were 7:1 (Mergesort), 18:1 (MultiWave, $K=16$), and 15:1 (WaveFront, $K=16$). While higher local memory to cache ratios would make the point more convincingly, the hit rates indicate that a small operand cache is surprisingly effective. This is attributable in large measure to the locality of reference preserved by the hybrid execution model.

Parallelism

Given a cache size of 64x4 on a single processor and LIFO queue discipline, the question of how well the realistic machine can exploit parallelism remains. This section presents the results of running a 10x10 matrix multiplication with the number of processors as the independent variable. The example is necessarily small due to the performance limitations of the emulator. It is significant only to note that parallelism can indeed be exploited, even on a small example.

Table 5-8: Realistic Parallelism			
Processors	Critical Path	Average Parallelism	Hit Rate
1	33,457	0.8	58.5
2	17,137	1.6	58.5
4	9,069	3.0	57.7
8	4,751	5.8	55.8
10	3,919	7.0	55.9
16	2,616	10.6	56.0
32	1,734	15.9	58.7

The table shows critical path, average parallelism[57], and aggregate cache hit rate. Figure 5-4 depicts the speedup (ratio of single-processor execution time to the execution time on n processors). In all cases, the number of aborted instructions was less than 3,648 (13.2% of successful instructions), and run length was consistently 3.7.

Recall that the optimal hit rate for the matrix multiplication benchmark on a single processor was found to be 63.5% by a previous experiment. Using this as a basis, the effective hit rates in this experiment are approximately 90%.

Toleration of Latency

Table 5-9: Effect of Latency			
Processors	Critical Path	Average Parallelism	Hit Rate
32, L=10	1,899	14.5	59.6

No amount of "optimization" by packing instructions into larger chunks is worth much if it negates the architecture's ability to synchronize efficiently or to tolerate latency. It is reasonably clear that the hybrid architecture provides the necessary synchronization support at a basic level for the purposes of program decomposition. But what about the hybrid machine's tolerance of long latency operations?

The effect of physical partitioning, or distributing a program can be estimated by assigning a higher than unit latency cost to each inter-codeblock communication. Specifically, each codeblock-to-codeblock com-

---

[57]A low value here reflects low parallelism, a significant number of aborted instructions, or both.

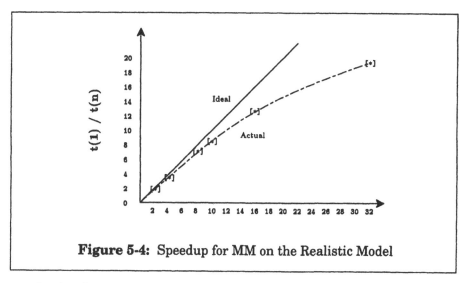

Figure 5-4: Speedup for MM on the Realistic Model

munication incurs communication latency L (ignoring locality), **STOR** instructions incur latency[58] cost L, and **LOAD** instructions incur latency cost
$2L$.

Figure 5-5 shows the effect of unit latency on the 10×10 example, with
K=11. In Figure 5-6, the inter-processor latency has been increased to 10
pipe steps, yet the increase in critical path time is only 9.52%. Two forms
of parallelism have made this masking possible: first, multiple continuations are available on any one processor due to K-unfolding of loops.
Second, each continuation contributes an average of half a run length's
number of instructions to the pool of executable instructions at any given
time.

5.3 SUMMARY

This chapter has demonstrated the benefits of the hybrid architecture
which argue for its superiority over von Neumann machines as the basis
for a scalable, general-purpose parallel computer:

• **Synchronization:** Efficient synchronization mechanisms al-

---

[58]Recall that the latency is attributable to the time between instructions and not time
within an instruction.

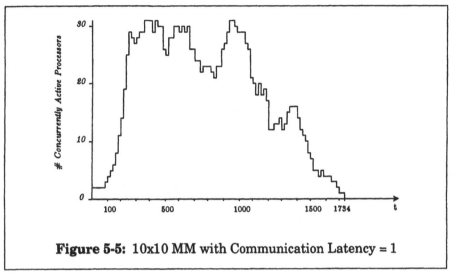

Figure 5-5: 10x10 MM with Communication Latency = 1

low the exploitation of the same kinds of parallelism as on a
dataflow machine, yet implicit synchronization is possible
within a single thread. It has been shown that the architecture is capable of iteration unfolding and inter-procedural
parallelism wherein the synchronization is not at all simple
and straightforward, but rather requires a fine-grained approach.

• **Latency Toleration:** The same synchronization mechanisms
allow parallelism to mask latency.

An underlying theme of the hybrid architecture is that the cost of exploiting parallelism should be manifest and should not be masked by the architecture as it is in the dataflow regime. This belief shows itself in explicit **FORK** instructions and in loop unfolding costs. Given that this architecture provides considerable leverage for reducing the critical path
time of the body of a given inner loop, some re-thinking of compilation
strategies along the lines of unfolding outer loops and mapping inner loops
to a small number of properly-ordered SQ's is indicated.

It has been shown that, although the hybrid instruction set is less powerful than the TTDA instruction set, instruction counts are comparable,
leading to the conclusion that the full synchronization generality of the
TTDA can indeed be compiled into some amount of program-counter based
synchronization.

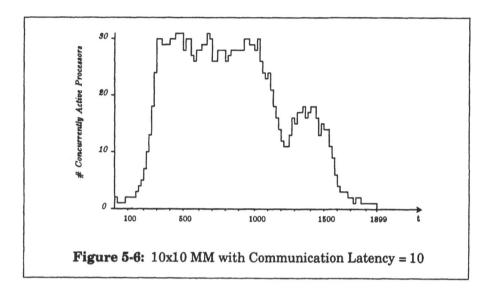

Figure 5-6: 10x10 MM with Communication Latency = 10

Considerable work remains in evaluating and characterizing this architecture. While preliminary studies have demonstrated that the hybrid architecture does indeed have better locality than a TTDA-like machine and that even very small caches can be used effectively to relieve the local memory bottleneck, additional study is required to make engineering-level decisions about pipeline balance, memory sizes, and so on.

Chapter Six

Conclusion

This study is concluded by reviewing the work done to date in unifying the dataflow and von Neumann views of computer architecture. The first section summarizes the the present work. The second section presents directions for future work. The last section analyzes related efforts by other researchers in light of the present work.

6.1 SUMMARY OF THE PRESENT WORK

The overall goal of this study has been to understand the critical hardware structures which must be present in any scalable, general-purpose parallel computer to effectively tolerate latency and synchronization costs. The main conclusion is that any such machine must execute a parallel machine language, having the following three characteristics:

- The execution time for any given instruction must be independent of latency. Traditional latency-sensitive operations, *e.g.*, LOADs from memory, must be re-phrased as split transactions which separately initiate an operation and later explicitly synchronize on the availability of the result.

- Each explicit synchronization event must be named. This implies efficient means for creating and re-using names as well as an efficient mechanism for enforcing synchronizing behavior based on the names. Names must be drawn from a large name space, and it must be possible to manipulate them as first-class hardware data types.

- Means for expressing both implicit and explicit synchronization must be provided. Implicit, *i.e.*, program counter based, synchronization provides the means for passing state between instructions within an unbroken thread. Explicit synchronization is necessary at the programming level in the exploitation of parallelism and at the machine level in the masking of latency.

In that neither von Neumann nor dataflow machines exhibit all three of these characteristics, a new architecture has been synthesized and analyzed. It has been demonstrated through emulation experiments and analysis of the model that the new architecture, based on the principles of PML, has the ability to exploit the same classes of parallelism as a dataflow machine. Consequently, the hybrid architecture can control communication latency cost through the exploitation of parallelism. Moreover, the cost of synchronization is low enough to allow its free an unencumbered use in decomposing programs for parallel execution.

From the standpoint of pure von Neumann architectures, the hybrid is evolutionary in the addition of a synchronizing local memory, split transaction memory operations, and a large synchronization name space. Synchronizing local memories and register sets are not new. Most noteworthy of the previous machines in this regard is the HEP [40, 41]. However, the scheme proposed in this study is more general than that of the HEP. Similarly, split transactions in and of themselves are not new, but the hybrid architecture shows the importance of inexpensive context switching as the primary means for making the most of split transactions.

The biggest departure from the traditional von Neumann architectural view is the introduction of large name spaces for synchronization purposes. In particular, the number of low-level synchronization names is limited only by the size of local memory. Further, the number of concurrently active threads is limited only by the number of meaningful continuations. In contrast, the HEP architecture allows only 64 processes per processor to be named simultaneously. From a hardware point of view, 64 processes is a sizable number. From the compiler's point of view, however, the number is far too small and implies that processes are a precious resource to be carefully managed. In the hybrid, this restriction is lifted. It could be argued that any small, fixed number of hardware processes could be virtualized by an added layer of interpretation, but the cost of such schemes in terms of lost time makes them unattractive. Large synchronization name spaces add the flavor of dataflow machines to von Neumann machines.

From the standpoint of pure dataflow architectures, the hybrid is evolutionary in that it adds the means for the compiler to exercise some explicit control over the pipeline. Because a thread holds the pipeline until it executes a potentially suspensive instruction, the entire machine state can be brought to bear on the problem of efficiently communicating information between instructions. In an abstract sense, the execution of the thread is atomic in that intermediate state changes in the processor are invisible outside the thread. This class of compiler-directed pipeline control is absent in both the TTDA and in Monsoon [46]. The hybrid further takes the stance that synchronization should be explicit as should forking of parallel activity. This simplification of the instruction set demonstrably does not drive the instruction count up in many cases because much of the forking and its attendant synchronization is superfluous. Even so, in the limiting case, the hybrid machine can still emulate instruction level dataflow with an instruction count expansion factor of no more than two, and arguably an identical cycle count. This leads to the observation that explicit synchronization instructions, used when necessary, may in some sense be cheaper than paying the full cost of synchronization at each instruction. This is, perhaps, the equivalent of the RISC argument applied to parallel computing.

In [8], the question of the possibility of "modifying" a von Neumann processor to make it a suitable building block for a parallel computer was raised. It was believed that the salient characteristics of a dataflow machine which made it a suitable building block were split-phase memory operations and the ability to context switch inexpensively. Given the addition of mechanisms like these, there was some lingering doubt as to what kind of synchronization efficiencies could be achieved and how much of the von Neumann architecture would be left. As presented in this study, engineering arguments regarding efficient implementation of PML's and the persistence of program counter based sequencing in the hybrid model have dispelled much of the doubt.

As yet unanswered is the question of the effectiveness of the hybrid architecture, or architectures like it, for other parallel programming models (e.g., Halstead's MultiLisp [31]); this is explored in more detail in Section 6.3. Of considerable practical interest is the possibility of targeting FORTRAN compilers to the hybrid paradigm.

6.2 FUTURE WORK

Opportunities for continuation of the present work abound, and are only outlined here.

- **Model:** This work investigates an architecture suitable for exploiting parallelism in single applications where all processors cooperate. Higher-level systems issues such as virtualization of the processor space and memory address space have not been considered for supporting multiprogramming and higher levels of tasking. It is believed that the right approach is to generalize the SQ mechanism upward to subsume higher-level tasks, but it is not clear how synchronization should be handled in the presence of dynamic address translation and demand paged memory.

- **Code Generation:** A number of schemes for improving dynamic instruction counts (*e.g.*, **RSTN** elimination in **LOOP**s when all sinks are in a single SQ, **TSTN** elimination in **SIGNAL-TREE**s for multiple sources from a single SQ, etc.) have been outlined but not implemented. It is reasonable that this work should be carried out by a peephole optimizer which operates on the partitioned graph. Such an idea has been considered but not developed in the present work. Also, techniques for register allocation need to be explored in the context of multiple, asynchronous readers. Optimizations such as the System/370 style **BXLE** instruction for decrementing, testing, and branching on an iteration variable are implementable in a straightforward way and need to be explored. Improvements to the **LOOP** implementation, *e.g.*, the overlapping of iteration area initialization with useful computation, have been outlined but not tested.

- **Machine Structure:** A number of optimizations remain unexplored, *e.g.*, reference-count slot resetting based on bounded fanout to make frames entirely self-cleaning and hardware support for tagged data (*e.g.*, trapping, autocoercion, etc.). The local memory presence bits should be generalized along the lines of Monsoon [46] such that each operand fetch or store can specify one of a fixed number of state-transition functions. Such a mechanism can perform the existing functions, *e.g.*, synchronizing and nonsynchronizing reads, nonstickiness, etc., as well as more sophisticated functions (*e.g.*, subsuming the flag bits of the iteration descriptor). Various engineering issues remain, especially in the area of implementing fast manager-call instructions (*e.g.*, **MKIS**, **GETC**).

6.3 RELATED WORK

This section explores related research efforts over the last 10 years or so. The common threads that bind these projects together are an understanding, at some level, of the two fundamental issues of latency and synchronization, and the beliefs that the von Neumann model is not sufficient, while the dataflow model is not necessary.

HEP Revisited

It is truly remarkable that the hybrid architectures under investigation today, including the present work, can trace so much of their low-level synchronization structure to the HEP. While the HEP was forced by its pipeline architecture to interleave at least eight execution contexts in order to keep the pipeline full, the present effort recognizes the deleterious effect this has on the working set size at the level of, say, an operand cache. It is believed that in order to support a spectrum of programming models from standard FORTRAN through the most highly parallelizable functional style, the ability to execute long sequential threads efficiently cannot be traded away. Moreover, unless the processor truly has nothing better to do, low-level busy waiting (*e.g.*, in the main pipeline and in the SFU pipeline) is wasteful of cycles. Nevertheless, an important place in the history of computer architecture is rightly reserved for the HEP as the first machine which made a genuine attempt to address the two fundamental issues. One could say that many new machines which follow its lead lie just beyond the horizon.

MASA Revisited

At first blush, it may appear that the restriction of one child process per context in MASA imposes a rather rigid restriction; however, it is possible to spawn, then detach, any number of children, relying on full/empty bits or futures for synchronization. In the hybrid model, a given codeblock can dynamically invoke any number of children, with all synchronization occurring through the various frames. This is more strongly similar to the action of MASA's notion of process creation, which requires allocation of futures for the passing of results. Tasks in MASA are clearly more than hybrid continuations in that they have private state, but they are less than codeblock invocations in that their private state is restricted to a small number of registers. There is, therefore, a not-too-surprising tradeoff between the cost of allocating lots of futures for the privilege of treating all child invocations as processes and the potential benefit of additional parallelism. One would clearly view the problem differently starting with an annotated MultiLisp program *vs.* starting with a dataflow program graph.

MASA provides the means for dynamic redistribution of work: the state of a task is easily transported because it is relatively small. The hybrid machine must make decisions about workload distribution at codeblock invocation time. It is not practical to consider picking up a hybrid codeblock invocation and moving it because of its size[59]. Moreover, all continuations for a single codeblock invocation must reside on a single processor.

The UCI Process-Oriented Model Project

Bic at the University of California, Irvine, has been investigating methods of exploiting the apparent inefficiencies in dataflow systems by systematically eliminating dynamic synchronization operations [12]. His technique is based on translating graphs into sets of linear sequences of instructions. To the extent that the sequences contain more than a single instruction, dynamic synchronization is eliminated. His partitioning method is depthfirst: Repeatedly apply this algorithm until the graph is empty:

- Initialize a new (empty) partition.

- Select and remove an instruction from the graph, called *inst*, which has the property that it receives no input from any instruction in the codeblock.

- Repeat while *inst* has an output used by some other instruction in the codeblock:

    - Add *inst* to the partition.

    - Remove *inst* from the graph.

    - Select one of *inst*'s outputs. *Inst* now becomes the instruction denoted by this output.

- Add *inst* to the partition.

- Remove *inst* from the graph.

---

[59]Inter-codeblock naming is not a problem, however, because all inter-codeblock interactions happen with fully qualified names via the **MOVR** instruction.

The execution paradigm is as follows: program memory contains a suitable representation of codeblocks as collections of partitions. Invocations are named according to U-Interpreter rules [5] with the exception that the statement (instruction) number s is divided into $s1$, naming a partition, and $s2$, naming an instruction within a partition. In contrast to the dataflow model where triggering is based on exact matching of activity names, names are matched associatively ignoring the $s2$ field. This is another way of saying that a partition is the unit of schedulability.

An associative waiting/matching store implements this mechanism, but much more is expected of it than simply associative matching. Each entry uniquely denotes an instance of a partition, contains a missing token count, and maintains a pointer to a list of tokens which have arrived for the instance. As tokens arrive for a given instance and which specify $s2=0$ (*i.e.*, they are headed for the first instruction), the count is decremented. Until it reaches zero, tokens are accumulated in the list. When it reaches zero, there are sufficient tokens to execute at least one instruction in the partition. At this time, the actual instantiation of the partition takes place which involves copying a blank template of the code from program memory to execution memory. In the process, tokens in the list are merged with the code — values are stored into the appropriate operand slots. A process control block is created and entered into an array of such control blocks in the processor.

This model is interesting but may exhibit some implementation difficulties. From experience with Id graphs, one would expect a large number of very small partitions. Moreover, experience with the TTDA has shown that, as a program's invocation tree is explored eagerly, the partially-computed state left behind as the wave of control proceeds toward the leaves is enormous. These two facts lead to the belief that the size of the PCB "register" array may have to be of a size which is comparable to execution memory in order to avoid frequent deadlock. Moreover, copy operations (with merging) are implied for each and every invocation. Assuming execution memory is not multiported, this will represent a tremendous number of cycles in which no useful computing can take place. In contrast, the hybrid model does not copy code and, to the extent that code can be generated to leave frames clean, invocation is inexpensive.

It is not at all clear what implications the depth-first partitioning method will have on the operand working set size and how this will compare to breadth-first techniques such as MDS. The author is most interested in seeing the analytic and/or experimental results as they are produced. It is clear, however, that depth-first partitioning will rely heavily on pipeline bypassing since, by definition, instruction n depends on the output of instruction $n-1$.

The IBM/ETH Project

Buehrer at ETH Zurich and Ekanadham at IBM Yorktown have developed a model for a hybrid machine which is remarkably similar to the present work. Details have been published elsewhere [15, 16, 26] and are only summarized here.

The authors assume a shared memory load/store multiprocessor of conventional origins augmented with features as follows:

- **Local Memory with Presence Bits:** Each processor has a memory to which it alone has access, and that each slot in said memory has state bits indicating *full*, *empty*, or *awaited*.

- **Send/Receive Instructions:** The instruction set supports a notion of one processor SENDing an instruction to either another processor or to a global memory unit. Received message/instructions are executed asynchronously. LOAD messages are an example — an address from which to load, and a tag are sent from the initiating processor to the appropriate destination.

- **Explicitly Split Read Transactions:** The IREAD instruction, given a LOCAL-ADDR and a GLOBAL-ADDR, resets the presence bit at LOCAL-ADDR and builds a SEND which will read GLOBAL-ADDR, return it to LOCAL-ADDR, and awaken any processes waiting on it.

- **Tag-to-Process Mapper:** Rather than having local processes busy-wait once a long-latency operation has been started, process state can be evacuated from the processor, and an identifier <LOCAL-ADDR,*Process*> can wait in an associative memory. The completion of the long-latency operation will include searching the memory for identifiers with matching LOCAL-ADDRs. The processes so denoted will be extracted and re-enabled for execution.

Based on these primitives, it is shown that I-Structure storage can be synthesized and, using I-Structures, producer-consumer parallelism can be exploited.

Their proposal for partitioning a dataflow graph involves coloring all primary input nodes in the graph with a single color, and each local-memory synchronizing read instruction (the target of a dynamic arc) with a separate color. For the remaining nodes, color is inherited as follows:

- If all of its immediate predecessors of color c, the node inherits color c.

- Otherwise, the node is assigned a totally new color.

Nodes with the same color form a sequential segment. In execution, all of these segments share access to the execution state of the codeblock. It is a simple matter to prove that MDS will always produce the same number or fewer SQ's than Buehrer and Ekanadham (B+E) will; consider the common case of two instructions which each depend on the same set of dynamic arcs. MDS will create a single SQ containing these instructions while B+E will create two, each containing a single instruction. This will tend to drive down the mean run length.

In the hybrid model, reawakening of tasks is expedited by storing the continuation of the suspended SQ into the empty frame slot. In the B+E model, associative matching is proposed with the attendant reliance on the size and cost of such a memory. They have recognized, however, the possibility of storing process identifiers directly into empty local slots when it can be guaranteed that there will never be more than a single reader.

There are other, less significant differences in the approaches. In B+E, a **LOAD** turns into two instructions, one to initiate and one to synchronize, while in the hybrid paradigm, the synchronization is always folded forward into the instruction which will use the value. In B+E, registers may be considered valid across suspensions, necessitating a means to save and restore them. In the hybrid approach, the maintaining of state in registers across potential suspensions is forbidden so as to eliminate the need for state saving. The issue here is much deeper than whether a compiler can be organized to do this — it is clear that it can. The issue is one of performance. The present work makes the statement that it is better to invest in operand cache technology than in register save/restore technology. It has been demonstrated through the experiments that this can be done, but it places a premium on reducing the working set size at the operand level.

6.4 CLOSING REMARKS

It is truly encouraging and exciting to see the harmony in all of the efforts aimed at combining von Neumann and dataflow architectures. The author fully expects that somewhere among all of these projects is the key to practical scalable, general-purpose parallel computing. All of these new efforts owe much to the language-based studies of the dataflow model pioneered by Arvind and Dennis over the last 20 years. But, just as importantly, these efforts seek to reconcile the apparent benefits with the tremendous base of knowledge surrounding the von Neumann model, *viz.*, instruction set design, compilation, and optimization.

Neither von Neumann architecture nor dataflow architecture alone can achieve the goal of scalable, general purpose parallel computing.

With the hybrid perspective, there is great hope.

References

[1]   Anderson, D. W., F. J. Sparacio, and R. M. Tomasulo.
        The IBM System/360 Model 91: Machine Philosophy and
            Instruction-Handling.
        IBM Journal 11:8-24, January, 1967.

[2]   Arvind, S. A. Brobst, and G. K. Maa.
        Evaluation of the MIT Tagged-Token Dataflow Architecture.
        Computation Structures Group Memo 281, MIT Laboratory for
            Computer Science, Cambridge, MA 02139, December, 1987.

[3]   Arvind and D. E. Culler.
        Dataflow Architectures.
        Annual Reviews of Computer Science 1:225-253, 1986.

[4]   Arvind and K. Ekanadham.
        Future Scientific Programming on Parallel Machines.
        In *Proceedings of the International Conference on Supercomputing.*
            Athens, Greece, June, 1987.

[5]   Arvind and K. P. Gostelow.
        The U-Interpreter.
        Computer 15(2):42-49, February, 1982.

[6]   Arvind and R. A. Iannucci.
        Instruction Set Definition for a Tagged-Token Data Flow Machine.
        Computation Structures Group Memo 212-3, MIT Laboratory for
            Computer Science, Cambridge, MA 02139, December, 1981.

[7]   Arvind and R. A. Iannucci.
        A Critique of Multiprocessing von Neumann Style.
        In *Proceedings of the 10th Annual International Symposium on
            Computer Architecture.* June, 1983.

[8]   Arvind and R. A. Iannucci.
        Two Fundamental Issues in Multiprocessing.
        In Proceedings of DFVLR - Conference 1987 on *Parallel Processing
            in Science and Engineering.* Bonn-Bad Godesberg, June, 1987.

[9]   Arvind, R. S. Nikhil, and K. Pingali.
        Id Nouveau Reference Manual, Part II: Operational Semantics.
        Technical Report, MIT Laboratory for Computer Science, April,
            1987.

[10]   Arvind, R. S. Nikhil, and G. M. Papadopoulos.
        Results from the MIT Tagged-Token Dataflow Project.
        August, 1987.
        Computation Structures Group Internal Memorandum.

[11]   Bell, C. G.
        Private Communication.
        1988.

[12]   Bic, L.
        A Process-Oriented Model for Efficient Execution of Dataflow
            Programs.
        In *Proc. of the 7th International Conference on Distributed
            Computing*. Berlin, West Germany, September, 1987.

[13]   Block, E.
        The Engineering Design of the STRETCH Computer.
        In *Proceedings of the EJCC*, pages 48-59. 1959.

[14]   Bouknight, W. J., S. A. Denenberg, D. E. Mcintyre, J. M. Randall,
        A. H. Sameh, and D. L. Slotnick.
        The ILLIAC IV System.
        Proceedings of the IEEE 60(4), April, 1972.

[15]   Buehrer, R. and K. Ekanadham.
        Dataflow Principles in Multi-processor Systems.
        Technical Report, ETH, Zurich, and Research Division, Yorktown
            Heights, IBM Corporation, July, 1986.

[16]   Buehrer, R. and K. Ekanadham.
        Incorporating Data Flow Ideas into von Neumann Processors for
            Parallel Execution.
        IEEE Transactions on Computers C-36(12):1515-1522, December,
            1987.

[17]   Censier, L. M. and P. Feautrier.
        A New Solution to the Coherence Problems in Multicache Systems.
        IEEE Transactions on Computers C-27(12):1112-1118, December,
            1978.

[18] Cox, G. W., W. M. Corwin, K. K. Lai, and F. J. Pollack.
Interprocess Communication and Processor Dispatching on the Intel 432.
ACM Transactions on Computer Systems 1(1):45-66, February, 1983.

[19] Culler, D. E.
Resource Management for the Tagged-Token Dataflow Architecture - S.M. Thesis.
Technical Report 332, MIT Laboratory for Computer Science, Cambridge, MA 02139, January, 1985.

[20] Culler, D. E.
Managing Parallelism and Resources in Scientific Dataflow Programs.
PhD thesis, MIT Department of Electrical Engineering and Computer Science, May, 1989.

[21] Deminet, J.
Experience with Multiprocessor Algorithms.
IEEE Transactions on Computers C-31(4):278-288, April, 1982.

[22] Dennis, J. B.
First Version of a Data Flow Procedure Language.
In B. Robinet (editor), *Lecture Notes in Computer Science.* Volume 19: *Programming Symposium: Proceedings, Colloque sur la Programmation*, pages 362-376. Springer-Verlag, 1974.

[23] Dennis, J. B.
Data Flow Supercomputers.
Computer 13(11):48-56, November, 1980.

[24] Eckert, J. P., J. C. Chu, A. B. Tonik & W. F. Schmitt.
Design of UNIVAC - LARC System: 1.
In *Proceedings of the EJCC*, pages 59-65. 1959.

[25] Edler, J., A. Gottlieb, C. P. Kruskal, K. P. McAuliffe, L. Rudolph, M. Snir, P. J. Teller & J. Wilson.
Issues Related to MIMD Shared-Memory Computers: The NYU Ultracomputer Approach.
In *Proceedings of the 12th Annual International Symposium On Computer Architecture*, pages 126-135. IEEE Computer Society, Boston, June, 1985.

[26] Ekanadham, K.
Multi-Tasking on a Dataflow-like Architecture.
Technical Report RC 12307, IBM T. J. Watson Research Laboratory, Yorktown Heights, NY, November, 1986.

[27]   Ellis, J. R.
       Bulldog: a Compiler for VLIW Architectures.
       The MIT Press, 1986.

[28]   Fisher, J. A.
       Very Long Instruction Word Architectures and the ELI-512.
       In *Proc. of the 10th, International Symposium on Computer
           Architecture.* IEEE Computer Society, June, 1983.

[29]   Fujita, T.
       *A Multithreaded Processor Architecture for Parallel Symbolic
           Computing.*
       Technical Memo 338, MIT Laboratory for Computer Science,
           Cambridge, MA 02139, September, 1987.

[30]   Gurd, J. R., C. C. Kirkham, and I. Watson.
       The Manchester Prototype Dataflow Computer.
       Communications of the ACM 28(1):34-52, January, 1985.

[31]   Halstead, R. H., Jr.
       MultiLisp: A Language for Concurrent Symbolic Computation.
       ACM Transactions on Programming Languages and Systems
           7(4):501-538, October, 1985.

[32]   Halstead, R. H., Jr., and T. Fujita.
       MASA: A Multithreaded Processor Architecture for Parallel Sym-
           bolic Computing.
       In *Proceedings of the 15th Annual International Symposium on
           Computer Architecture.* IEEE Computer Society, Honolulu,
           Hawaii, June, 1988.

[33]   Heller, S. K.
       An I-Structure Memory Controller (ISMC).
       S. M. Thesis, MIT Department of Electrical Engineering and Com-
           puter Science, Cambridge, MA 02139, JUNE, 1983.

[34]   Heller, S. K. and Arvind.
       *Design of a Memory Controller for the MIT Tagged-Token Dataflow
           Machine.*
       Computation Structures Group Memo 230, MIT Laboratory for
           Computer Science, Cambridge, MA 02139, October, 1983.
       Proceedings of IEEE ICCD '83 Port Chester, NY.

[35]   Hennessy, J. L.
       VLSI Processor Architecture.
       IEEE Transactions on Computers C-33(12):1221-1246, December,
           1984.

[36]   Hiraki, K., S. Sekiguchi, and T. Shimada.
        System Architecture of a Dataflow Supercomputer.
        Technical Report, Computer Systems Division, Electrotechnical
            Laboratory, Japan, 1987.

[37]   Iannucci, R. A.
        High Performance Memory System Utilizing Pipelining Techniques.
        U.S. Patent 4,685,088, IBM Corporation, P.O. Box 6, Endicott, NY
            13760, August, 1987.

[38]   *IBM System/370 Principles of Operation*
        IBM Corporation, 1984.
        GA22-7000.

[39]   Johnsson, T.
        Lambda Lifting.
        Workshop on Sequential Implementations of Functional Languages.
        Chalmers Institute Of Technology, Goteborg, Sweden, 1985.

[40]   Jordan, H. F.
        Performance Measurement on HEP - A Pipelined MIMD Computer.
        In *Proceedings of the 10th Annual International Symposium On
            Computer Architecture*, pages 207-212. IEEE Computer
            Society, Stockholm, Sweden, June, 1983.

[41]   Kowalik, J. S.
        *Scientific Computation Series: Parallel MIMD Computation: HEP
            Supercomputer and Its Applications.*
        The MIT Press, 1985.

[42]   Kuck, D., E. Davidson, D. Lawrie, and A. Sameh.
        Parallel Supercomputing Today and the Cedar Approach.
        Science Magazine 231:967-974, February, 1986.

[43]   Li, Z. and W. Abu-Sufah.
        A Technique for Reducing Synchronization Overhead in Large
            Scale Multiprocessors.
        In *Proc. of the 12th, International Symposium on Computer
            Architecture*, pages 284-291. IEEE Computer Society, June,
            1985.

[44]   McCarthy, J., P. W. Abrahams, D. J. Edwards, T. P. Hart, and
            M. I. T. Levin.
        LISP 1.5 Programmer's Manual.
        MIT Press, Cambridge, MA, 1965.

[45] Moon, D. A.
      Architecture of the Symbolics 3600.
      In *Proceedings of the 12th Annual International Symposium On
          Computer Architecture*, pages 76-83. IEEE Computer Society,
          Boston, June, 1985.

[46] Papadopoulos, G. M.
      Implementation of a General Purpose Dataflow Multiprocessor.
      PhD thesis, MIT Department of Electrical Engineering and Com-
          puter Science, July, 1988.

[47] Patterson, D. A.
      Reduced Instruction Set Computers.
      Communications of the ACM 28(1):8-21, January, 1985.

[48] Radin, G.
      The 801 Minicomputer.
      In *Proceedings of the Symposium on Architectural Support for Pro-
          gramming Languages and Operating Systems*. ACM, March,
          1982.
      Same as Computer Architecture News 10,2 and SIGPLAN Notices
          17,4.

[49] Rau, B., D. Glaeser, and E. Greenwalt.
      Architectural Support for the Efficient Generation of Code for
          Horizontal Architectures.
      In *Proceedings of the Symposium on Architectural Support for Pro-
          gramming Languages and Operating Systems*. March, 1982.
      Same as Computer Architecture News 10,2 and SIGPLAN Notices
          17,4.

[50] Russell, R. M.
      The CRAY-1 Computer System.
      Communications of the ACM 21(1):63-72, January, 1978.

[51] Sarkar, V., and J. Hennessy.
      Partitioning Parallel Programs for Macro Dataflow.
      In *Proceedings of the ACM Conference on Lisp and Functional
          Programming*, pages 202-211. ACM, August, 1986.

[52] Smith, B. J.
      A Pipelined, Shared Resource MIMD Computer.
      In *Proceedings of the 1978 International Conference on Parallel
          Processing*, pages 6-8. 1978.

[53]   Terman, C. J. and S. A. Ward.
        The L Architecture.
        May, 1985.
        Internal Report, Real-Time Systems Group, MIT Laboratory for
            Computer Science, Cambridge, MA 02139.

[54]   Thornton, J. E.
        Parallel Operations in the Control Data 6600.
        In *Proceedings of the SJCC*, pages 33-39. 1964.

[55]   Tomasulo, R. M.
        An Efficient Algorithm for Exploiting Multiple Arithmetic Units.
        IBM Journal 11:25-33, January, 1967.

[56]   Traub, K. R.
        *A Compiler for the MIT Tagged-Token Dataflow Architecture - S.M.
            Thesis.*
        Technical Report 370, MIT Laboratory for Computer Science,
            Cambridge, MA 02139, August, 1986.

[57]   Traub, K. R.
        A Dataflow Compiler Substrate.
        Computation Structures Group Memo 261, MIT Laboratory for
            Computer Science, Cambridge, MA 02139, March, 1986.

[58]   Traub, K. R.
        Sequential Implementation of Lenient Programming Languages.
        PhD thesis, MIT Department of Electrical Engineering and Com-
            puter Science, May, 1988.

[59]   *ALTO: A Personal Computer System - Hardware Manual*
        Xerox Palo Alto Research Center, Palo Alto, California, 94304,
            1979.

Index

I

194

T

U